WHAT'S INSIDE?

7 SCIENCE

14 MATHEMATICS, IT AND COMPUTING

18 ENGINEERING AND BUILDING MANAGEMENT

24 SOCIAL SCIENCE

32 ARTS, CREATIVE ARTS AND HUMANITIES

41 BUSINESS AND ADMINISTRATIVE STUDIES

EMPLOYMENT REVIEW

WRITTEN BY CHARLIE BALL

The graduate jobs market in 2016

At the beginning of 2016, the outlook for the graduate jobs market looked reasonably positive. The market for first degree graduates seemed to be completing a recovery from the last recession and the economy had bounced back to the point where there were clear signs of a shortage of graduates in many important occupations, notably in nursing, engineering, teaching, IT and parts of the business services industry.

What did 2014/15 graduates do?

This is how last year's graduates fared when leaving university. *See graph 1.*

The most recent DLHE data reveals a graduate job market in sound shape. 312,330 first degrees were awarded to UK-domiciled graduates last year, down by 25,900 on 2014, and the majority, 76.4%, were working after six months.

Unemployment was at 5.7%, a significant fall from 6.3% in 2015. Early unemployment rates below 6% are a sign of a relatively good jobs market for graduates and only one year since 2000 – the pre-recession employment peak in 2007 – has had a lower early graduate unemployment rate. Employment rates for all major subjects were up on the previous year.

Types of employment

Most main areas of graduate-level employment took a greater share of the labour market in 2015 and non-graduate employment was down across the board. However, as the number of graduates fell substantially, so did the number entering employment – 189,245 graduates from 2015 are known to have been in work after six months compared with 199,810 from 2014, the highest on record.

As fewer graduates went into work in 2015, almost all areas of non-graduate employment saw fewer graduates entering them – and so did many areas of graduate employment. This may be one reason why many sectors reported difficulty finding enough graduates to employ in 2015, most notably in engineering, construction, information technology and computing, health, education and business support. It looks likely that these areas will continue to experience shortages of graduates for the near future, and indeed throughout 2016, as businesses continue to report difficulties in recruiting them in the same sectors that struggled last year.

Most graduates who were working six months after leaving university were employed on permanent contracts, 15% were on fixed-term contracts lasting at least a year – much the largest group here were junior doctors – and 3% of graduates were on zero-hours contracts, primarily in non-graduate employment such as retail, waiting and bar work and the care industry. Self-employment and freelancing was much more common in the arts and creative industries than in other sectors, but there were significant groups of graduates in education and IT who also worked for themselves.

As mentioned, the figures show a graduate employment market in relatively good health and one where a number of areas saw graduates in significant demand from employers. Year on year the UK has been creating large numbers of new jobs for graduates and that looks set to continue. Data from the Annual Population Survey shows that by the end of 2015, there were 370,500 more individuals working in graduate employment than at the end of 2014, with particularly large rises in science, technology and engineering, business and finance, and management positions.

Where do graduates work?

Most graduates work either near to where they went to university or they go home and find work there. Graduates in general do not tend to move to a location they have no ties to in order to get a job. Even in London, only 35% of graduates who started work in the capital were neither from the city nor had studied there.

The graduate jobs market is mainly associated with the larger cities. One in five graduates – over 41,000 – started their career in London and many more went to work in the commuter belt around London with another 22,500 getting work in South East England.

However, not all graduate jobs are in that region. Birmingham was the most popular destination for those not working in London with 4,155 graduates starting their careers there. Manchester, Leeds, Glasgow, Edinburgh, Oxford, Liverpool, Belfast, Bristol and Cardiff all employed at least 2,000 graduates each last year, as did the regions of Hertfordshire, Kent, Surrey, Lancashire and Essex. In general, UK cities have the infrastructure and high-skilled employment opportunities to support a wide

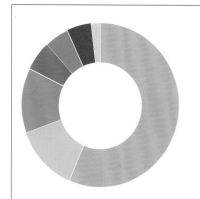

OUTCOMES FOR 2014/15 GRADUATES AFTER SIX MONTHS

Working in the UK	56.5%
In further study, training or research	13.1%
Working part-time in the UK	12.9%
Unemployed, including those due to start work	5.7%
Working and studying	5.1%
Other	4.9%
Working overseas	1.8%

Graph 1

range of graduates. Those looking for work may need to consider working in the larger cities to maximise their chances.

WHERE DID 2015 GRADUATES WORK?

Leeds 3,430
Manchester 3,740
City of London 3,890
Birmingham 4,155
Westminster 6,145

Further study

When the economy improves, the proportion of graduates going into postgraduate study on completion of their first degree tends to fall, but 2016 bucked that trend. 18.2% of first-degree graduates were either solely studying or taking a course as well as working after six months. This was up from 17.6% the year before, possibly as a result of the introduction of a new system of loans for postgraduate study. Nearly half of those going into further study (49%) took a degree that went straight into a taught Masters qualification, popular subjects being psychology, management, sports science, business, finance, law, computing or marketing.

Another 18.6% of those taking a further qualification went into teacher training, and 12% embarked on a research doctorate, with chemistry, physics, maths, biology and computing being the most common options. Science subjects are usually favoured at doctoral level as many careers in science, particularly in research and development at universities or in business, require a doctorate to enter.

The impact of Brexit and future outlook

On June 23rd the referendum on membership of the European Union (EU) resulted in a vote to leave. Business was, in the main, agreed that this outcome would lead to a more difficult jobs market.

Even as 2016 began, some employers were giving thought to the contest and taking a cautious stance towards recruitment in anticipation of the referendum. Once the result came in, business confidence dropped sharply and although it made a partial recovery in the late summer, the process of actually leaving the EU had not yet begun. This affects all discussions of the graduate jobs market because until the process is formally launched, and possibly for some time after that, business will be uncertain about the timing and outcome of the departure. This uncertainty makes business reluctant to make major decisions on their future and therefore has an impact on hiring.

But although there is likely to be a downturn in the graduate jobs market as the process of leaving the EU takes place, the UK is and will remain a wealthy nation with a strong demand for highly skilled people.

The graduate jobs market was in reasonable health earlier in 2016 and while it may experience disruption in the next few years, it will recover in time.

The country is about to enter a prolonged period where the number of 18 year olds – and thus the pool from which prospective students are drawn – is due to fall significantly year on year. This is likely to last well into the next decade, meaning there is no guarantee that the number of new graduates entering the jobs market will continue to rise as it has consistently over the last two decades. Falls in graduate numbers, as happened in 2015, may become more common.

Last year the economy added 370,500 new jobs at graduate level. While this was an unusually large increase caused by a robust recovery for the graduate economy, over the last decade the UK has gained around 230,000 new graduate jobs a year even though that period was dominated by a severe recession. In addition, that figure does not consider replacement demand – the jobs freed up by other workers leaving the jobs market, usually through retirement.

Many of our skilled industries, particularly in manufacturing and construction, have an ageing workforce who will need replacing with skilled young workers as they retire over the next decade.

The way ahead is uncertain, but the economy's appetite for our graduates and question marks over whether as many young people will go to university as in previous years will ensure that most university graduates will continue to get jobs within months of leaving university. Most of those jobs will be relatively well-paid, permanent positions in professional roles.

Through their university careers services, students can access highly professional careers support with experience of aiding them in challenging economic times.

FIRST DEGREE GRADUATES FROM ALL SUBJECTS 2015

SURVEY RESPONSE: 79.3% | **FEMALE: 142,830** | **MALE: 104,985** | **TOTAL RESPONSES: 247,835** | **ALL GRADUATES: 312,330**

OUTCOMES SIX MONTHS AFTER GRADUATION

Working full time in the UK	56.5%
In further study, training or research	13.1%
Working part time in the UK	12.9%
Unemployed, including those due to start work	5.7%
Working and studying	5.1%
Other	4.9%
Working overseas	1.8%

TYPE OF COURSE FOR THOSE IN FURTHER STUDY

Masters (e.g. MA, MSc) 49.2%

Postgraduate qualification in education 18.6%

Doctorate (e.g. PhD, DPhil, MPhil) 12.0%

Other study, training or research 9.1%

Other postgraduate diplomas 6.5%

Professional qualification 4.6%

Total number of graduates in further study 32,385

TYPE OF WORK FOR THOSE IN EMPLOYMENT

Graduates who were in employment either full time, part time or working and studying in the UK

FEMALE: 108,565 | **MALE: 75,820** | **TOTAL IN EMPLOYMENT IN THE UK: 184,390**

Health professionals	16.7%
Retail, catering, waiting and bar staff	11.1%
Business, HR and finance professionals	10.2%
Marketing, PR and sales professionals	7.4%
Clerical, secretarial and numerical clerk occupations	6.8%
Education professionals	6.4%
Other occupations	6.1%
Arts, design and media professionals	5.9%
Childcare, health and education occupations	5.3%
Other professionals, associate professionals and technicians	5.2%
Legal, social and welfare professionals	4.9%
Engineering and building professionals	4.7%
Information technology (IT) professionals	4.4%
Managers	3.8%
Science professionals	1.1%
Unknown occupations	0.1%

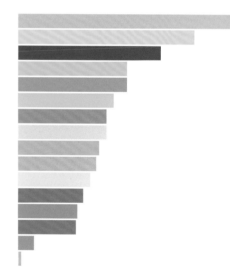

TOP TEN PROFESSIONAL AND MANAGERIAL JOBS HELD BY FIRST DEGREE GRADUATES IN EMPLOYMENT IN THE UK
% as total of first degree graduates who were employed in professional and managerial jobs in the UK

Nurses 10.4%

Primary and nursery education teaching professionals 5.1%

Medical practitioners 4.6%

Marketing associate professionals 4.1%

Business and related associate professionals n.e.c. 2.9%

Programmers and software development professionals 2.5%

Finance and investment analysts and advisers 2.2%

Human resources and industrial relations officers 2.1%

Chartered and certified accountants 1.9%

Pharmacists 1.7%

MYTHS ABOUT THE GRADUATE LABOUR MARKET

WRITTEN BY CHARLIE BALL

Over the years a great deal has been said in public about universities, graduates and the jobs market, and demand for degrees. Much of it is broadly accurate but nevertheless a number of myths and misconceptions persist. This article takes a brief look at the most common of these and examines the evidence around them.

'There are too many graduates'

As long as people in the UK have been going to university, others have complained that too many people have been getting degrees. At present the unemployment rate for new graduates is running at under 6% – a level that has been associated with good graduate jobs markets at least since the 1970s.

Over the whole population the unemployment rate for graduates runs at half the non-graduate rate and only just climbed over 4% in the last recession. Even young graduates between 21 and 30 who have just entered the jobs market are less likely to be unemployed than someone without a degree.

Of course, this could simply mean that graduates are all going to work in shops and call centres. However, in the 11 years from 2004, data from the Government's Annual Population Survey shows that the UK economy added over 2.5 million new jobs in managerial, professional and associate professional jobs – those roles seen as 'graduate' and those which are increasingly difficult for people without degrees to access.

This comes to more than 233,000 new jobs at 'graduate level' every year and that's before we even start to consider replacement demand, the vacancies opened up by people leaving the jobs market due to retirement and so on. That's why many parts of the graduate economy, especially in nursing, medicine, teaching, engineering and parts of the

business services and finance industries, reported serious shortages of graduates in 2015 as demand started to outstrip supply.

It is fair to say that we might better balance some aspects of graduate supply against demand by taking more account of which occupations and skills are in genuine shortage, so that students are better able to match their interests to where there are opportunities. However, it isn't obvious that we have too many people going to university.

'There are no jobs for graduates'

As mentioned above, the economy has been creating a healthy number of jobs for graduates. Most graduates every year get jobs, and the majority of graduates get full-time, permanent jobs. Last year nearly 190,000 new graduates are known to have found jobs in the UK and the large majority got jobs that require a degree or which would be very difficult to get without one.

But it is also true that some graduates struggle in the jobs market; graduate jobs are not spread evenly throughout industries and they are not found evenly around the country. They tend to be in industries associated with high skills, such as health, education, our large business and financial industry, science, engineering and the arts, and they tend to be concentrated in the larger cities.

Graduates who have a strong focus on only one or two industries, or who have their hearts set on working in a small range of places, will find it harder to find jobs. In a competitive jobs market, students need as much help as they can get to write good applications – visiting their university careers service is a must to give them the best possible chance of getting a good job.

'All the jobs are in London'

As mentioned, the graduate jobs market is concentrated in the cities; in fact many graduates see London as the only place that they can find jobs. It is easy to see why. One sixth of the UK population lives there, 22% of UK businesses are based there, and most major firms have their head offices there.

Yet only 21% of graduates start their career in the capital. Many of the larger cities have thriving jobs markets for graduates: Birmingham, Manchester, Glasgow,

Edinburgh, Leeds, Cardiff, Liverpool, Oxford, Belfast and Bristol all took at least 2,000 new graduate employees each last year. London is still the most important city for some jobs, but there are actually few jobs you can get in London that you absolutely cannot get elsewhere.

For graduates who – like the majority of young people – are concerned about the cost of living in London, there are other options available if they can put together a strong application.

'All the jobs are with big business'

A lot of attention is paid to the big graduate training schemes with large international firms. They are often very well paid and well structured, taking capable graduates and training them effectively.

However, they are not the right choice for everyone, and many very able young people work elsewhere. Some of us prefer the challenge of working for a smaller business; you tend to have more responsibility, a wider range of duties (and so opportunities to learn), and often a real say in the direction of the business.

Last year 35% of new graduates were working at companies with fewer than 250 employees, and one in five were with companies with fewer than 50. This shows that to find a rewarding and challenging role graduates don't always have to go through the big graduate schemes.

PREPARING GRADUATES FOR AN UNCERTAIN FUTURE

WRITTEN BY JANE HOWIE

When looking at the workplace of the future, the themes of uncertainty and chaos emerge regularly: how will it look, which roles will exist, and which skills will be required for individuals to be active members of the global workforce?

This has got me thinking: how do we as employability and career professionals prepare our graduates so that they can respond to the demands of industry tomorrow when we do not know what this future is going to look like?

This is a particularly relevant question to ask in the light of a recent 2016 World Economic Forum report[1], which indicated that more than one-third of the skills considered important in today's workforce will have changed considerably by 2020.

I believe that we can effectively future-proof our graduates by encouraging them to become borderless leaders[2]. This can be achieved through:

- embedding enterprise and entrepreneurship within the academic curriculum, nurturing the creation and enhancement of enterprising[3] skills such as strategic thinking, networking and opportunity seeking, and the flexibility to work across multiple disciplines creatively;
- engaging students with challenging coaching[4] that facilitates self-efficacy and the continuous practice of lifelong learning, whereby individuals can modify skillsets to deal effectively with new challenges and unfamiliar situations.

Many institutions are taking this on board, and embedding enterprise and entrepreneurship within the university curriculum. A good example of this is the University of Leicester's Transferable Skills

Framework[5] to which all employability activities are aligned. Institutions are building upon these frameworks and introducing social entrepreneurship activities in collaboration with corporate partners through initiatives such as the WildHearts' Micro-Tyco Business Challenge[6], which associates business excellence with economic justice and provides students with the opportunity to practise global business fundamentals while benefiting society. Other effective means of developing borderless leaders include engaging students in:

- project-based learning with real-world problems, where students collaborate with peers from other disciplines to achieve a solution;
- work-based learning that can extend to shadowing, mentoring, internships, where students are directly immersed in the challenges faced in the workplace.

These learning opportunities are geared towards replicating the uncertainties and challenges of the global workplace. Through its pedagogical design, the curriculum can prepare students for the future by providing them with immediate and future work competencies.

While these activities are individual learning opportunities in their own right, at the same time the diversity of the learning opportunities offered by a university's curriculum can reinforce the development of future-proof graduates as students can build their university experience based upon their career values and motivations, by combining university curriculum learning with real-life practice.

A second approach to developing borderless leaders is to engage students in challenging coaching. This builds upon the skillsets that the student has fostered via the curriculum and other experiences.

It acts as a tool they engage with to facilitate a growth mindset[7] where a habit of continuous lifelong learning and resilience is created. This enables those being coached to become accountable for their own actions and behaviours.

As employability and career professionals, we cannot predict with total certainty what will happen in the future but by fostering the

development of a growth mindset that commences when students are at university and continues into the workplace, we are future-proofing graduates with what's required to be successful.

This is because the students will be opening themselves up to opportunities where they can refine and re-calibrate their skills to deal with the uncertainties and challenges that they will no doubt face in the workplace.

As employability and career professionals, we can collaborate with academic colleagues in order to apply academic theory to practice. This can be achieved through sharing our expertise of the graduate recruitment market and employment trends, disseminating good practice with regard to skills development, or passing on our external contacts so that the curriculum reflects real life.

With regard to challenging coaching, we can provide academic colleagues with consultative advice on the delivery of activities which champion a mindset for continuous lifelong learning and resilience within the curriculum. This does mean, however, that we need to future-proof our practice and engage in continuous lifelong learning so that we are equipped to deal with the challenges of the workplaces of the future, and have the tools to support academics and students.

See references & resources on page 50

SCIENCE OVERVIEW

WRITTEN BY JANICE MONTGOMERY

Graduates in Science, Technology, Engineering and Maths (STEM) are widely regarded as critical to the UK economy[1], providing the impetus for new developments that will drive discovery in fields as wide as astronomy, technological innovation, healthcare and food science.

There are considerable differences between uptake in the various science disciplines and in their employment outcomes. This article examines the outcomes for science graduates in the cohort graduating in 2015, leaving the other STEM disciplines to be discussed elsewhere in this publication.

The UK Government's ten-year strategy for science and innovation, published in 2014, sets out a vision for improving STEM education in schools, a £5.9billion budget for capital science funding and the development of world-class laboratories to ensure the UK leads the way in scientific exploration and development[2]. A more recent report concerning graduate employment and accreditation in STEM[3] has drawn attention to the increasing numbers of pupils at school who are taking STEM subjects, leading to an increase in undergraduate numbers from 76,000 in 2006 to over 98,000 in 2015[4]. Despite dips in 2012-13, the first intake of students to pay full fees, the report makes clear that the numbers across science subjects, such as chemistry and physics, have been steadily increasing over the last ten years[5].

Destinations
The data provided by the Higher Education Statistics Agency (HESA) shows that science has maintained and slightly increased its share of the overall undergraduate population, standing at around 7.9%. This figure masks considerable change within individual subjects with biology, physical and geographical sciences and sports science all seeing a decline in graduating numbers, sports science in particular experiencing a drop of 1,400 students on the previous year. This could be attributed to being the first group to graduate from the entry cohort in 2012-13 who had to pay full fees and there is no doubt that that played a part in the overall reduction in new students that year and therefore graduates now.

However, physics is experiencing a positive resurgence with 400 additional students on the previous year and chemistry an extra 140. It is possible that in choosing subjects for study at undergraduate level, pupils (and parents) are influenced by the excellent rates of work and further study amongst previous graduates in these subjects, and in the more obvious correlation between study and vocational employment at a time when fee payment is sharpening the focus on return on educational investment.

Although science graduates have lower rates of immediate employment on leaving university, compared to the average of over 56% for all students, they also have much higher rates of further study demonstrating the demands of employers in science-related fields for graduates with higher level qualifications such as PhDs and Masters.

Chemistry and physics graduates in particular have higher levels of further study, outstripping the national average by around 20%, they also have extraordinarily high numbers of graduates who opt for extended study at PhD level; two thirds of graduates opt to do so compared to the national average of 12%. This reflects the opportunities for research and development in these fields and the support provided by the Higher Education Funding Councils across the UK for such research[6].

What kind of employment is pursued by science graduates?
The websites of the Royal Society for Chemistry, the Royal Society of Biology and the Institute for Physics all include careers sections that demonstrate the range of careers open to graduates of these disciplines[7]. For example, chemistry offers opportunities in science education, energy production, the environment, the research and development of household products and pharmaceuticals, biomedicine and quality assurance. It is therefore worth noting that only a relatively small percentage of science graduates become science professionals. Chemistry leads the way with nearly 19% of its graduates working as science professionals, followed by biology and physics, with fewer than 8% respectively. Broadly, this may very well be related to wider changes in science-related industry in the UK[8].

Although certain scientific giants such as GlaxoSmithKline and Pfizer remain, much research and development is taking place in small and medium enterprises (SMEs), which do not have the ability to recruit and train graduates in the same way as that being offered by, for example, the major accountancy firms.

Many science graduates start their careers as other associated professionals or science technicians; this is the choice of over 14% across the disciplines with the exception of physics, which is slightly lower at 8.5%.

There is also an oddity to be found in the very high percentage of graduates who become business and finance professionals instead of pursuing a career in science. Nearly 20% of all physicists choose this option as do 15% of chemists and 14% of graduates from the physical and geographical sciences. This is indicative of the correlation between the skills developed while studying science and the skills required for success in business related sectors.

As one might expect, large numbers of sports scientists (over 20%) become sports coaches or fitness instructors and over 12% of chemistry graduates secure employment in chemistry related roles. Beyond these expected outcomes there are significant numbers of graduates from each discipline who become business and marketing professionals, finance and investment analysts, management consultants, teachers and IT specialists.

A recent government paper[9] suggests that more can be done to embed careers advice and the development of work-ready skills among graduates in their science curricula, and that students themselves should take more responsibility for engaging at an early stage with their own career paths. The report indicated that greater engagement through the curriculum and through contact with careers services in universities may lead to an even wider range of employment for science graduates and minimise both un- and under-employment[10].

Unemployment
Given that there is a nationwide need for students with good science skills to populate research and development in the future, why do this year's statistics show higher levels of unemployment amongst science graduates than graduates as a whole?

The recently published Wakeham report suggests that there are several key factors for both un- and under-employment among science graduates. Employers are less concerned about where and what a graduate studied and much more concerned about their lack of soft skills, business awareness and industrial experience[11]. Not only are graduates lacking skills such as the ability to give presentations, manage projects, write reports and work in teams, but there are particular concerns about a lack of maths skills and most notably, a lack of adaptability and resilience[12].

The report points out that resilience in particular is vital while working in the interdisciplinary teams that are so common in these fields, as well as the need for an appreciation of profit motives, business planning and understanding clients' needs. Science students cannot change the face of industry but they can and ought to attempt to understand things like converging technologies, the growing diminution of natural resources, big data and the digitalisation of production. They also need to develop the soft skills outlined above while at university, which might enhance their employability when they come to graduate.

Gender divide
The gender divide continues to be a topic of some interest in science subjects. Physical and geographical sciences have the most evenly balanced gender split, followed by chemistry, but biological sciences show a predominance of women graduates while physics and sports science are heavily predominated by male graduates (2:1 male: female ratio in sports science and around 4:1 in physics).

A government report in 2014, 'Women in Scientific Careers', points out the pressing need for more personnel in science careers and by definition, more women.

It acknowledges the efforts expended by government to encourage more girls to study science at school which seem to be bearing fruit, but also points out that should women choose to pursue careers in pure science, these careers are still not compatible with family life and childrearing should women wish to combine the two.

The report focuses on academic careers but it should be noted that many women also make up the large numbers who go on to work in business, finance, marketing, sales and education where a work-life balance may be easier to maintain.

There continue to be organisations working very deliberately to increase the profile of women working in science[13] and thus the take up at university level, with the overall aim of increasing the number of women working in STEM positions in the UK by one million. Athena Swan awards[14] are changing the landscape of opportunities for women in science research and one would expect to see a growing impetus for change in future years.

Salaries
The salary range provided by respondents to the destinations survey is understandably broad across the disciplines. There are some disciplines where a high percentage of graduates have not yet established professional careers and perhaps are continuing the typical jobs students do such as bar work or retail (this accounts for 18.2% of biology graduates) – therefore, the salaries are a little lower than other sciences but still range from £17,000 to £21,600.

For subjects such as chemistry, where 76.3% obtain work in a professional or managerial role such as financial advisers or chemists, the salary range is a little higher at £18,400 to £25,600. Physics graduates are overall the best paid with salaries ranging from £17,700 to £28,400, reflecting the high numbers who enter employment as IT professionals or business, HR and finance professionals.

Salary information should only be used, however, as a very rough guide to outcomes. The destinations survey is conducted only six months after graduation when graduates are often in lower paid positions with a view to gaining the experience they require to progress in their chosen career. For example, physical and geographical graduates may take positions as ecological surveyors or countryside rangers, which are not as well paid as becoming a graduate accountant but

will stand them in good stead if they then wish to become an environmental consultant.

The future
While demand for science graduates remains high, the prospects are good for those who choose to study science at university level. Although there are challenges in encouraging more women to study subjects such as physics and sports science, and having studied to then remain in pure science fields[15] there is a far broader challenge for universities, careers staff and the students themselves to ensure engagement in early career planning, skills development and employment awareness.

This will put science graduates in a position to take advantage of the very wide range of opportunities open to them at the end of their undergraduate study.

See references & resources on page 50

BIOLOGY GRADUATES FROM 2015

SURVEY RESPONSE: 81.4% | **FEMALE: 2,480** | **MALE: 1,705** | **TOTAL RESPONSES: 4,185** | **ALL GRADUATES: 5,140**

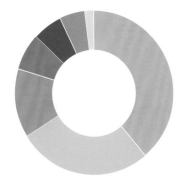

OUTCOMES SIX MONTHS AFTER GRADUATION

Working full time in the UK	39.0%
In further study, training or research	27.2%
Working part time in the UK	13.6%
Unemployed, including those due to start work	7.2%
Other	6.1%
Working and studying	4.9%
Working overseas	1.9%

TYPE OF COURSE FOR THOSE IN FURTHER STUDY

Masters (e.g. MA, MSc) 50.5%
Doctorate (e.g. PhD, DPhil, MPhil) 22.0%
Postgraduate qualification in education 12.3%
Other study, training or research 10.6%
Other postgraduate diplomas 4.1%
Professional qualification 0.5%
Total number of graduates in further study 1,140

EXAMPLES OF COURSES STUDIED

MSc International Health Policy
MSc Ecology, Evolution and Conservation
MSc Forensic Science
MSc Pharmacology
MBCHB

PhD Genome Stability
PhD Cancer Research
PGCE Primary
PGDE Science
BA Professional Studies in Tax
PGDip Physician's Assistant

TYPE OF WORK FOR THOSE IN EMPLOYMENT

Graduates who were in employment either full time, part time or working and studying in the UK

FEMALE: 1,455 | **MALE: 950** | **TOTAL IN EMPLOYMENT IN THE UK: 2,405**

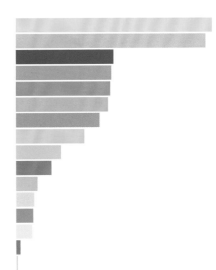

Retail, catering, waiting and bar staff	18.2%
Other professionals, associate professionals and technicians	17.6%
Business, HR and finance professionals	9.1%
Numerical clerk, clerical and secretarial occupations	8.9%
Other occupations	8.8%
Childcare, health and education occupations	8.6%
Science professionals	7.8%
Marketing, PR and sales professionals	6.4%
Education professionals	4.2%
Managers	3.3%
Health professionals	2.0%
Arts, design and media professionals	1.7%
Information technology (IT) professionals	1.6%
Legal, social and welfare professionals	1.5%
Engineering and building professionals	0.4%
Unknown occupations	0.1%

EXAMPLES OF 2015 BIOLOGY GRADUATE JOB TITLES AND EMPLOYERS (SIX MONTHS AFTER GRADUATION)

Trainee manager - Aldi
Royal naval officer - Royal Navy
Biology teacher - secondary school
Fraud operations agent - Paypal
Tax associate - PwC
Analyst - Morgan Stanley
Accountant - EY
Sales executive - Diageo
Marketing assistant - higher education

Research officer - national park
Science technician - water company
Apprentice brewer - brewery
Ecological surveyor - Thomsons
Civil Service fast stream - Civil Service
Healthcare assistant - NHS
Medical sales rep - pharmaceutical company
Administrator - environmental agency

Waiter - Pizza Express
Sales assistant - Moshulu
Chalet host - ski company

CHEMISTRY GRADUATES FROM 2015

SURVEY RESPONSE: 84.2% | **FEMALE: 1,295** | **MALE: 1,805** | **TOTAL RESPONSES: 3,095** | **ALL GRADUATES: 3,680**

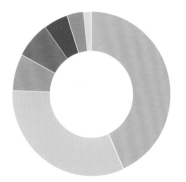

OUTCOMES SIX MONTHS AFTER GRADUATION

Working full time in the UK	43.5%
In further study, training or research	32.1%
Working part time in the UK	7.4%
Unemployed, including those due to start work	7.1%
Other	5.0%
Working and studying	3.5%
Working overseas	1.4%

TYPE OF COURSE FOR THOSE IN FURTHER STUDY

Doctorate (e.g. PhD, DPhil, MPhil) 60.3%

Masters (e.g. MA, MSc) 19.3%

Postgraduate qualification in education 12.6%

Other study, training or research 4.4%

Other postgraduate diplomas 2.9%

Professional qualification 0.6%

Total number of graduates in further study 995

EXAMPLES OF COURSES STUDIED

MSc Medicinal Chemistry

MSc Polymer, Colour and Fine Chemicals

MSc Science and Technology Policy

PhD Chemistry

PhD Materials Science and Metallurgy

PGDE Secondary

TYPE OF WORK FOR THOSE IN EMPLOYMENT

Graduates who were in employment either full time, part time or working and studying in the UK

FEMALE: 730 | **MALE: 950** | **TOTAL IN EMPLOYMENT IN THE UK: 1,680**

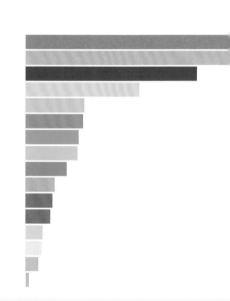

Science professionals	18.9%
Other professionals, associate professionals and technicians	18.6%
Business, HR and finance professionals	15.7%
Retail, catering, waiting and bar staff	10.4%
Marketing, PR and sales professionals	5.4%
Other occupations	5.3%
Clerical, secretarial and numerical clerks	4.9%
Education professionals	4.8%
Information technology (IT) professionals	3.8%
Childcare, health and education occupations	2.7%
Managers	2.5%
Engineering and building professionals	2.3%
Arts, design and media professionals	1.6%
Legal, social and welfare professionals	1.5%
Health professionals	1.2%
Unknown occupations	0.3%

EXAMPLES OF 2015 CHEMISTRY GRADUATE JOB TITLES AND EMPLOYERS (SIX MONTHS AFTER GRADUATION)

Supply chain manager - KPMG

Teacher - Teach First

Chemical analyst - ALMAC

Graduate scientist - AstraZeneca

Research scientist - Lhasa Ltd

Nuclear engineer - EDF

Software engineer

Risk analyst - J.P. Morgan

Junior consultant - PwC

Trader - Deutsche Bank

Publishing assistant - publishing house

Exhibitions intern - art gallery

Chorister - cathedral choir

Ministry trainee - Church of England

Civil Service fast stream - Foreign and Commonwealth Office

Bookseller - Waterstones

Bar staff - football club

Carbon management assistant - higher education

Carpenter's assistant - scenery production company

PHYSICAL AND GEOGRAPHICAL SCIENCES GRADUATES FROM 2015

SURVEY RESPONSE: 82.2% | **FEMALE: 1,295** | **MALE: 1,425** | **TOTAL RESPONSES: 2,720** | **ALL GRADUATES: 3,310**

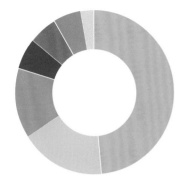

OUTCOMES SIX MONTHS AFTER GRADUATION

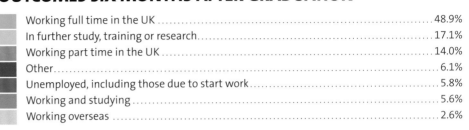

Working full time in the UK	48.9%
In further study, training or research	17.1%
Working part time in the UK	14.0%
Other	6.1%
Unemployed, including those due to start work	5.8%
Working and studying	5.6%
Working overseas	2.6%

TYPE OF COURSE FOR THOSE IN FURTHER STUDY

Masters (e.g. MA, MSc) 61.0%
Postgraduate qualification in education 21.4%
Doctorate (e.g. PhD, DPhil, MPhil) 6.9%
Other study, training or research 5.3%
Other postgraduate diplomas 4.0%
Professional qualification 1.5%
Total number of graduates in further study 465

EXAMPLES OF COURSES STUDIED

MSc River Basin Dynamics
MSc Energy and the Environment
MSc Meteorology
MSc Global Urban Justice
MSc Property
MSc Micropaleontology

MA Music and Sonic Media
PhD Environmental Engineering
PGCE Teach First
PGDE Secondary
HNC Music

TYPE OF WORK FOR THOSE IN EMPLOYMENT

Graduates who were in employment either full time, part time or working and studying in the UK

FEMALE: 870 | **MALE: 985** | **TOTAL IN EMPLOYMENT IN THE UK: 1,855**

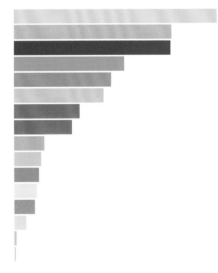

Retail, catering, waiting and bar staff	18.8%
Other professionals, associate professionals and technicians	14.6%
Business, HR and finance professionals	14.5%
Clerical, secretarial and numerical occupations	10.2%
Other occupations	9.0%
Marketing, PR and sales professionals	8.3%
Managers	6.1%
Engineering and building professionals	5.4%
Childcare, health and education occupations	2.8%
Education professionals	2.5%
Information technology professionals	2.3%
Legal, social and welfare professionals	2.1%
Science professionals	1.9%
Arts, design and media professionals	1.1%
Health professionals	0.2%
Unknown occupations	0.1%

EXAMPLES OF 2015 PHYSICAL AND GEOGRAPHICAL GRADUATE JOB TITLES AND EMPLOYERS (SIX MONTHS AFTER GRADUATION)

Recycling manager - council
Ecologist - JCA
Hydrometry assistant - environmental agency
Hydraulic modeller - Mott McDonald
Software support - investment company

Commercial analyst - Morrisons
Graduate trainee - Lloyds Bank
Investment manager - Smith and Williamson
Marketing graduate - Fujitsu
Choir director - university
Events producer - events company

Outdoor instructor - field centre
Countryside warden - council
Church intern - independent church
Barista - Starbucks
Sales assistant - Cotswolds

PHYSICS GRADUATES FROM 2015

SURVEY RESPONSE: 83.8% | **FEMALE: 535** | **MALE: 2,080** | **TOTAL RESPONSES: 2,615** | **ALL GRADUATES: 3,120**

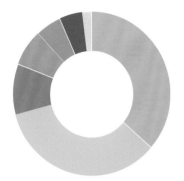

OUTCOMES SIX MONTHS AFTER GRADUATION

Working full time in the UK	36.6%
In further study, training or research	34.5%
Unemployed, including those due to start work	9.9%
Working part time in the UK	7.3%
Working and studying	5.1%
Other	4.9%
Working overseas	1.7%

TYPE OF COURSE FOR THOSE IN FURTHER STUDY

Doctorate (e.g. PhD, DPhil, MPhil) 60.6%
Masters (e.g. MA, MSc) 24.3%
Postgraduate qualification in education 10.2%
Other study, training or research 3.1%
Other postgraduate diplomas 1.7%
Professional qualification 0.2%
Total number of graduates in further study 900

EXAMPLES OF COURSES STUDIED

PhD Engineering
PhD Condensed Matter
MSc Automotive Engineering
MSc Tribology
MSc Diagnostic Imaging
MSc Particle Physics
MSc Cosmology

PGCE Science
PGDE Maths
GDL Law

TYPE OF WORK FOR THOSE IN EMPLOYMENT

Graduates who were in employment either full time, part time or working and studying in the UK

FEMALE: 270 | **MALE: 1,010** | **TOTAL IN EMPLOYMENT IN THE UK: 1,280**

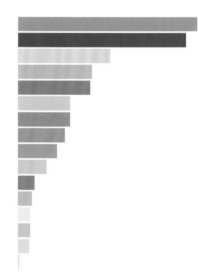

Information technology professionals	20.5%
Business, HR and finance professionals	19.2%
Retail, catering, waiting and bar staff	10.6%
Other professionals, associate professionals and technicians	8.5%
Engineering and building professionals	8.3%
Education professionals	6.0%
Science professionals	6.0%
Other occupations	5.4%
Clerical, secretarial and numerical clerks	4.5%
Marketing, PR and sales professionals	3.3%
Managers	1.9%
Childcare, health and education occupations	1.6%
Legal, social and wefare professionals	1.5%
Health professionals	1.4%
Arts, design and media professionals	1.3%
Unknown occupations	0.1%

EXAMPLES OF 2015 PHYSICS GRADUATE JOB TITLES AND EMPLOYERS (SIX MONTHS AFTER GRADUATION)

- Physics teacher
- Planner - Transport for London
- Graduate engineer - building company
- Network developer - BAE
- Software engineer - Thales
- Innovation analyst - intellectual property company

- Trainee - Barclays Bank
- Analyst - EY
- Product manager - manufacturing company

- Product control analyst - Centrica
- Patent attorney - Boult Wade
- Ski resort worker

SPORTS SCIENCE GRADUATES FROM 2015

SURVEY RESPONSE: 77.8% | **FEMALE: 2,495** | **MALE: 4,895** | **TOTAL RESPONSES: 7,390** | **ALL GRADUATES: 9,505**

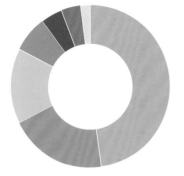

OUTCOMES SIX MONTHS AFTER GRADUATION

Working full time in the UK	46.3%
Working part time in the UK	19.3%
In further study, training or research	17.4%
Working and studying	7.1%
Other	4.3%
Unemployed, including those due to start work	3.8%
Working overseas	1.7%

TYPE OF COURSE FOR THOSE IN FURTHER STUDY

Masters (e.g. MA, MSc) 40.7%
Postgraduate qualification in education 40.1%
Other postgraduate diplomas 7.2%
Other study, training or research 7.0%
Doctorate (e.g. PhD, DPhil, MPhil) 4.1%
Professional qualification 0.9%
Total number of graduates in further study 1,290

EXAMPLES OF COURSES STUDIED

MSc Biomedical Sciences
MSc Sports, Business and Management
MSc Physiotherapy
MSc Biomechanics
MSc Biological Sciences
MA Sports Coaching

MA Journalism
PGDE Physical Education
PGCE Primary
BSc Physiotherapy

TYPE OF WORK FOR THOSE IN EMPLOYMENT

Graduates who were in employment either full time, part time or working and studying in the UK

FEMALE: 1,755 | **MALE: 3,620** | **TOTAL IN EMPLOYMENT IN THE UK: 5,370**

Other professionals, associate professionals and technicians	22.8%
Retail, catering, waiting and bar staff	16.0%
Other occupations	11.5%
Childcare, health and education occupations	9.9%
Education professionals	8.2%
Business, HR and finance professionals	5.9%
Health professionals	5.7%
Marketing, PR and sales professionals	5.3%
Clerical, secretarial and numerical clerks	5.3%
Managers	4.7%
Legal, social and welfare professionals	2.4%
Science professionals	1.0%
Information technology professionals	0.6%
Engineering and building professionals	0.4%
Arts, design and media professionals	0.4%
Unknown occupations	0.1%

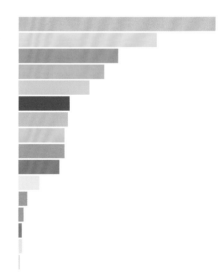

EXAMPLES OF 2015 SPORTS SCIENCE GRADUATE JOB TITLES AND EMPLOYERS (SIX MONTHS AFTER GRADUATION)

Physiotherapist assistant - NHS
Pre-registration pharmacist - NHS
Sports therapist - football club
Teacher - Teach First
P.E teacher - secondary school
Youth worker - lads' club
Support worker - council
Residential welfare officer - charity

Web designer - self employed
Trainee accountant - council
Estate agent
Journalist - sports magazine
Sports camps coordinator
Fitness instructor - Army
Teaching assistant - secondary school

Medical claims assistant - legal firm
Sales assistant - Morrisons
Barista - Starbucks
Tour manager - sports travel company
Driver - chemical company
Kitchen builder - Howdens

MATHEMATICS, IT AND COMPUTING OVERVIEW

WRITTEN BY GARETH HILL

The data from HESA's Destinations of Leavers from Higher Education (DLHE) survey 2014/15 shows two subjects with a diverse range of destinations for UK-domiciled, first degree graduates:

- IT and computing is a vocationally-oriented discipline and this is reflected in the fact that almost two-thirds (65.2%) of graduates went into full-time work in the UK following graduation compared to just under half (48.9%) of maths graduates.
- Maths graduates are much more likely to pursue further study (22.1%) than those from IT and computing (7.3%).
- Both disciplines have a higher unemployment rate (maths 7.2%, and IT and computing 9.9%) compared with all graduates (5.7%).

This article focuses on what maths and IT and computing graduates are doing after their degree, and what they can do while at university to develop their employability.

Mathematics
Maths graduates who enter employment in the UK primarily work in business, HR and finance professions (41.8%). They tend to take on roles that use their analytical and numeracy skills, such as finance and investment analysis/advice or chartered and certified accountancy. The next most likely employment destinations are in IT and education.

Maths graduates are much more likely to go onto further study (22.1%) than all graduates (13.1%). Almost a third of those in further study choose to study a postgraduate qualification in education. This is not surprising given the higher paying bursaries available to maths graduates who start a PGCE. The highest proportion of graduates choosing further study opt for a Masters (36.2%), with courses ranging from applied

mathematics to robotics. The salaries of maths graduates in full time work in the UK range from £18,000 to £29,000.

The Wakeham Review
The Wakeham Review[1] of STEM Degree Provision and Graduate Employability finds that maths graduates have a lower than average progression rate into professional-level jobs. In addition, the report identifies a number of themes cutting across STEM graduate employability, including:

- The importance of graduates gaining work experience. Research from the UK Commission for Employment and Skills' (UKCES) Employer Perspectives Survey states that relevant work experience is rated by two-thirds of recruiting employers (66%) as being a critical or significant criterion that they looked for in candidates.
- The value that employers place on 'work ready skills' and their perception that many graduates do not possess these skills. These skills, also known as 'soft skills', can include the ability to give presentations, commercial awareness, adaptability and a commitment to continuing professional development. These 'soft skills' are a foundation of what employers expect from graduates.
- Some employers have found that some graduates lacked the necessary resilience expected of them. They stated that having a graduate making mistakes in a new role is not in itself problematic. Indeed, they emphasised that in the workplace graduates need to be able to learn from failure and adapt their approach to ensure future success – but some graduates seemed unable to take disappointment on the chin.
- Graduates have a lack of awareness and understanding about how the skills they have gained during their degree relate to the current jobs market.

IT and Computing
The DLHE survey suggests a 'two tier' labour market within IT for graduates, with some doing extremely well but with others struggling – 65.2% are in full time employment in the UK while 9.9% are unemployed. Due to the vocational nature of IT and computing courses, most graduates choose to go directly into employment in the UK mainly in the information technology professions (60.8%). The most common jobs

for graduates are as programmers, software developers or web designers. Salaries for graduates range from £18,000 to £30,000.

In each of the last six years, more students have begun computer sciences courses than physics, chemistry and maths combined.

The Shadbolt Review
The Shadbolt Review[2] addresses the issue of unemployment among computer science graduates. The DLHE data shows unemployment at 10%, which is much higher compared with all graduates. The overall picture, however, is more complicated as computer science students who are in employment are more likely to be in graduate level work and well paid.

Those who take a sandwich course enjoy much lower levels of unemployment (6%) than those who don't (15%). Graduates from sandwich courses are twice as likely to be earning more than £20,000 compared with those who completed a standard degree.

Of those computer science graduates who are employed, one quarter of them are in London while the others are mainly located in the South East, East Midlands, Manchester and Leeds.

The UKCES report[3] that reviewed the requirement for high-level STEM skills (2015) found that the top three industries for IT professionals were:

- information and communication (36%);
- professional services (17%);
- financial services (9%).

What skills do employers want from IT graduates?
While many employers find that computer science graduates are well prepared for work, there remains a bloc of opinion that more could be done to develop graduates' skills and work readiness. As part of the Shadbolt review, employers were asked what skills IT graduates should possess to best meet their needs. The most common answers were:

- computer science specific skills, e.g. programming languages;
- soft skills, including communication;
- project management skills.

Some employers reject the need for graduates to know particular programming languages, arguing that the key thing that they look for is the ability to learn and select what is relevant based upon the task rather than simply to know the latest language.

Future trends
The UKCES Sector Insights report (2015) anticipates the following trends:

- the growing importance of cyber security;
- mobile and cloud computing;
- new applications of social media;
- collaborative platforms.

What careers are available to maths, IT and computing graduates?
There are a wide range of careers open to maths, IT and computing graduates. While it is good to be able to use the skills gained from your degree, it is important that graduates don't feel constrained by it when considering possible careers. For example, some students feel that if they complete a maths degree then they must go on to a 'maths-based career' such as accountancy or auditing. This isn't the case. It's important that graduates consider their strengths and what they are passionate about before considering their career options. Their university careers team can help them with this.

The evidence from the Shadbolt Review suggests that many students are unaware of the range of careers and types of employer that make up the labour market, often only applying to the high profile sectors and employers. It is worth students looking into a range of careers and employers to see which best matches with their skills and values. The best way to start doing this is by attending employer events at university and using the careers service.

The value of work experience
The evidence from both the Shadbolt and the Wakeham reviews suggests that maths/IT students would be well advised to plan what work experience they will be gaining during their university studies.

This evidence is further supported by the longitudinal study into the value of work experience, Futuretrack[4]. The two main objectives of this project were:

- to examine factors associated with students participation in paid and unpaid work;
- to study the effect of different forms of work experience on their development of skills and progress into the labour market following HE.

The results show that the transitions made by students into the labour market are influenced by the work experience they undertake while studying. In particular, respondents who had undertaken no work experience during study were less likely to have made a successful transition into the labour market than those who had undertaken some form of work experience. Most crucially, respondents who had undertaken both work-related learning and paid work had notably lower odds of unemployment and higher odds of self-confidence in comparison to respondents who had undertaken no work.

This is supported by the findings of The Graduate Market in 2015 (the High Fliers report)[5]:

'Almost half of the recruiters who took part in the research repeated their warnings from previous years – that graduates who have no previous work experience at all are unlikely to be successful during the selection process and have little or no chance of receiving a job offer for their organisations' graduate programmes.'

Develop a 'portfolio of experience'
The evidence from the Futuretrack study confirms the value of gaining experience. Schemes such as 'a Year in Industry' as part of your degree can be valuable, but other forms of work such as volunteering or a part-time job also have value. It's important that students develop a 'portfolio of experience' during university.

How to find work experience
According to Futuretrack, the most common way for graduates to find paid work is either through previously having worked for an employer or through applications to companies, either directly or in response to a job advert. Fifteen per cent of students did not undertake paid work while studying.

This suggests that in order for graduates to maximise their chances of gaining experience it helps if they:

- Are pro-active — opportunities are out there being open-minded and optimistic is important. Employers respond well to initiative.
- Use a variety of strategies — in addition to applying for advertised placements, students should also use their social network (friends, family etc.) and look at other ways to gain experience. Investigating different opportunities at the same time and then weighing them up is an effective way of making decisions about the future.
- Are resilient and persevere — to develop a 'portfolio of experience' students need to stick at it and not give up when setbacks come their way. They should be encouraged to have confidence in their ability.

How can students develop employability skills during their degree?
The key message from the evidence presented here is to undertake work experience. Students may decide to look for a course that offers a year in industry or for work placements during holiday periods. Students should follow the tips discussed in this article to develop a 'portfolio of experience'. They can do this by:

- developing the 'soft skills' that employers need through their studies, part time work or volunteering;
- planning their next steps carefully. Students need to be pro-active in their career development by gaining experience and taking part in employability sessions.
- reviewing their own resilience and considering a plan of how they could develop this during their degree. Being prepared to learn from failure, and to use it to help to develop themselves;
- researching into careers and organisations that interest them. They shouldn't be constrained by jobs that relate directly to their degree and should use their time at university to research careers and build a network;
- engaging with their careers service, taking part in workshops and talking one-to-one with their careers team at university.

These actions will put them in a stronger position to articulate their skills to employers, and help them to move into a career which best meets their needs.

See references & resources on page 50

MATHEMATICS GRADUATES FROM 2015

SURVEY RESPONSE: 82.3% | **FEMALE: 1,970** | **MALE: 2,990** | **TOTAL RESPONSES: 4,965** | **ALL GRADUATES: 6,030**

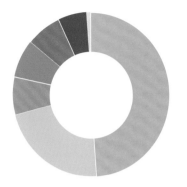

OUTCOMES SIX MONTHS AFTER GRADUATION

Working full time in the UK 48.9%
In further study, training or research 22.1%
Working part time in the UK 7.5%
Working and studying 7.4%
Unemployed, including those due to start work 7.2%
Other 5.7%
Working overseas 1.1%

TYPE OF COURSE FOR THOSE IN FURTHER STUDY

Masters (e.g. MA, MSc) 36.2%
Postgraduate qualification in education 30.4%
Doctorate (e.g. PhD, DPhil, MPhil) 23.4%
Other postgraduate diplomas 5.8%
Other study, training or research 2.6%
Professional qualification 1.5%
Total number of graduates in further study 1,095

EXAMPLES OF COURSES STUDIED

MSc Statistics
MSc Artificial Surveillance
MSc Quantity Surveying
MPhil Data Science
PhD Mathematics

PhD Applied Mathematics
PGCE Secondary Maths
TEFL (Teaching English as a Foreign Language)

TYPE OF WORK FOR THOSE IN EMPLOYMENT

Graduates who were in employment either full time, part time or working and studying in the UK

FEMALE: 1,300 | **MALE: 1,865** | **TOTAL IN EMPLOYMENT IN THE UK: 3,165**

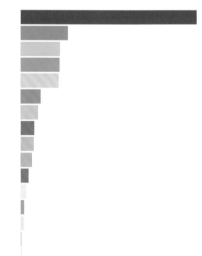

Business, HR and finance professionals 41.8%
Information technology (IT) professionals 12.3%
Education professionals 10.2%
Clerical, secretarial and numerical clerks 8.1%
Retail, catering, waiting and bar staff 7.9%
Other occupations 3.6%
Marketing, PR and sales professionals 3.6%
Managers 2.8%
Other professionals, associate professionals and technicians 2.8%
Childcare, health and education occupations 2.2%
Engineering and building professionals 1.9%
Legal, social and welfare professionals 0.8%
Science professionals 0.8%
Arts, design and media professionals 0.8%
Health professionals 0.3%
Unknown occupations 0.1%

EXAMPLES OF 2015 MATHEMATICS GRADUATE JOB TITLES AND EMPLOYERS (SIX MONTHS AFTER GRADUATION)

Graduate line manager - Royal Mail
Teacher - Teach First
Research engineer - QinetiQ
Traffic engineer - Transport for London
Pedestrian modeller - Mott Mcdonald
Web designer - university

Actuarial analyst - HSBC
Trainee accountant - BDO
Consultant - Deloite
Statistician - NHS
Visitor host - Warner Bros studio tour
Maths graduate assistant - primary school
Medical records clerical assistant - NHS
Accountancy administrator - local police finance department
Intern - local church

Store assistant - Game
Sales advisor - Ted Baker
Waitress - Bella Italia
Fishmonger/butcher - Tesco

COMPUTER SCIENCE AND IT GRADUATES FROM 2015

SURVEY RESPONSE: 79.5% | **FEMALE: 1,595** | **MALE: 8,070** | **TOTAL RESPONSES: 9,665** | **ALL GRADUATES: 12,155**

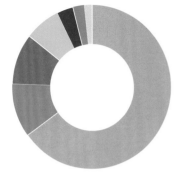

OUTCOMES SIX MONTHS AFTER GRADUATION

Working full time in the UK	65.2%
Working part time in the UK	10.5%
Unemployed, including those due to start work	9.9%
In further study, training or research	7.3%
Other	3.4%
Working and studying	2.3%
Working overseas	1.4%

TYPE OF COURSE FOR THOSE IN FURTHER STUDY

Masters (e.g. MA, MSc) 56.4%

Doctorate (e.g. PhD, DPhil, MPhil) 14.6%

Postgraduate qualification in education 12.2%

Other study, training or research 10.3%

Other postgraduate diplomas 5.4%

Professional qualification 1.1%

Total number of graduates in further study 705

EXAMPLES OF COURSES STUDIED

MSc Computer Science

MSc Advanced Computing

MSc Information Technology Management

PGCE Secondary Computer Science and Information Technology Education

PGCE Further Education

TYPE OF WORK FOR THOSE IN EMPLOYMENT

Graduates who were in employment either full time, part time or working and studying in the UK

FEMALE: 1,225 | **MALE: 6,305** | **TOTAL IN EMPLOYMENT IN THE UK: 7,530**

Information technology professionals	60.8%
Retail, catering, waiting and bar staff	9.4%
Business, HR and finance professionals	6.2%
Other occupations	5.5%
Clerical, secretarial and numerical clerk occupations	3.5%
Arts, design and media professionals	2.7%
Managers	2.7%
Marketing, PR and sales professionals	2.4%
Other professionals, associate professionals and technicians	2.2%
Education professionals	1.5%
Engineering and building professionals	1.2%
Childcare, health and education occupations	0.8%
Legal, social and welfare professionals	0.4%
Science professionals	0.3%
Health professionals	0.3%
Unknown occupations	0.2%

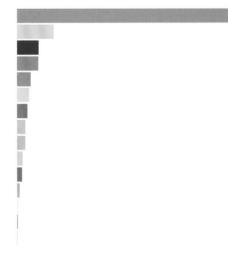

EXAMPLES OF 2015 COMPUTER SCIENCE AND IT GRADUATE JOB TITLES AND EMPLOYERS (SIX MONTHS AFTER GRADUATION)

CEO of start-up company

Team manager - Marks & Spencer

Trainee manager - Wetherspoon's

Ethical hacking lecturer - university

Paralegal - solicitors firm

Self-employed software designer - IT company

Cyber security analyst - security company

Junior developer - IT company

Software engineer - Foreign Office

Adviser - KPMG

Self-employed musician

Personal trainer - Virgin Active

Dental nurse - Dentists

HR administrator - NHS trust

Custody officer assistant - police force

Customer adviser - Sky

Bar staff - golf club

Security guard - magistrate's courts

ENGINEERING AND BUILDING MANAGEMENT OVERVIEW

WRITTEN BY BARRIE GRAY

The 2014/15 Destination of Leavers from Higher Education (DLHE) survey indicates that 16,125 or 5.2% of all UK domiciled first degree graduates study civil, mechanical or electrical and electronic engineering or architecture and building subjects. These disciplines form part of the Science, Technology, Engineering and Mathematics (STEM) subjects 'which are central to UK growth and have an important role in developing and contributing to the technical and scientific innovation that will drive the next generation of high value products, services and the burgeoning information and data-driven economy'[1].

Overall, there is a very high demand for engineers and scientists[2], which contributes to high levels of professional and managerial employment in both discipline-specific vocations (such as civil engineering) and fields related to the skills developed during these types of study, such as finance careers or software development.

Despite this significant demand, vacancies remain difficult to fill, particularly in engineering where employers struggle to recruit up to 60% of vacancies due to a lack of skills. This means that despite a shortage of graduates, levels of unemployment can be high among these disciplines. According to the recently released Wakeham report[3] students have not embraced careers advice while at university, gained appropriate work experience or sought to develop key skills such as business awareness, enterprising skills, project management, team working, report writing, adaptability and personal resilience.

So what of specific disciplines within the broad heading of engineering and building management? The following narrative provides an analysis of the DLHE survey for 2014/15 graduates and commentary on the outcomes for the subject areas:

- architecture and building;
- civil engineering;
- electrical and electronic engineering
- mechanical engineering.

Architecture and building
Of the 4,935 respondents to the DLHE survey, 79.2% are engaged in employment, which is slightly down on 2013/14 levels (79.7%). Of those employed in the UK, the most likely occupations are architectural and town planning technicians (19.3%), quantity surveyors (16.9%), chartered surveyors (9.4%) and architects (8.7%).

The predominance of graduates in employment as engineering and building professionals (nearly 50% of those in employment in the UK) is directly related to the high proportion of students who study architecture and building subjects. These subjects are vocationally orientated so it is expected that higher numbers of gradates will go on to undertake employment in professions directly related to their degree.

According to the Royal Institute of British Architects (RIBA)[4] those who study architecture tend to go into entry occupations that have further training attached, which explains the 19.3% of graduates who go into technician level roles.

The percentage of graduates who go into further study has increased slightly on 2013/14 (5.4%) to 6.6% and conversely the percentage of those working and studying has dropped from 6.2% in 2013/14 to 5.3% in 2014/15. This is likely to be due to an increase in specialist full time further study courses, such as façade engineering.

Unemployment has remained constant at 5.3%, perhaps reflecting the range of opportunities for graduates in a stable construction industry with increases in home building and ongoing major infrastructure projects such as Crossrail, HS2 and upgrading to 'smart motorways'[5]. There is also an increase in worldwide construction[6], which may make the UK's globally recognised degree programmes an asset for any graduates considering working overseas.

Civil engineering
Of the 2,325 respondents to the DLHE survey, 78.4% are engaged in employment, which is slightly higher than graduates from 2013/14.

This indicates a stable flow of graduate jobs for a discipline where 61% of graduates find employment in the UK as civil engineers and a further 14.2% find work in other engineering and building professions. This is not unexpected as, like architecture and building, civil engineering is a vocational programme that normally attracts students with a relatively clear career path in mind. While civil engineer is the most popular job title among 2014/15 graduates working in the UK, others have found work in developing fields with example job titles including graduate modeller and territory manager.

The percentage of graduates engaging in further study has again increased slightly from 8.7% in 2013/14 to 9.1% in 2014/15. This may be due to an increase in specialist further study qualifications aimed at specific jobs such as Masters-level study in project management and geo-environmental engineering. The percentage of civil engineering graduates choosing further study is lower than the national average of 13.1%, which is unsurprising given that most civil engineering degrees will lead to professional or managerial employment without the need for further study.

Unemployment fell slightly from 5% in 2013/14 to 4.8% for 2014/15 graduates. This is to be expected given the annual 'Engineering in Employment'[7] report shows a continued shortage of skilled civil engineers.

Electrical and electronic engineering
Of the 2,285 respondents to the DLHE survey, 75.7% are engaged in employment representing an increase from 73.6% in 2013/14 despite the overall national level of employment for all graduates remaining fairly static. This is most likely to be the result of the range of opportunities open to graduates from this discipline. Only 22% of these graduates in 2014/15 went into the electrical or electronic engineering professions. Graduates also embrace other professions including positions as programmers and software development professionals (9%), design engineers (7%) and other engineering professionals (7%).

The percentage of graduates engaged in further study has remained fairly stable at 9.7% for 2014/15 graduates, compared with 10.4% in 2013/14. There has been more of a drop in those engaged in work and study from 3.6% in 2013/15 to 2.7% in 2014/15. This may be the result of an increase in higher education institutions offering integrated Masters courses. Of those entering further study it is predominantly at Masters level in courses that may help them find specialist employment, such as information and digital forensics, and robotics.

Unemployment has fallen marginally from 8.9% for 2013/14 graduates to 8.3% for 2014/15 graduates, although this is still much higher than the national figure for all 2014/15 first degree graduates (5.7%). Given the vocational nature of the electrical and electronic degree programmes and the high levels of employment this seems surprising. However, degrees that are aimed at particular vocations do tend to lead to those not finding work in a related profession being more likely to be unemployed. This could be due to the fact that they will continue to look for work in their chosen field rather than take other unrelated work. However, it may represent the lack of skills outlined in the Wakeham report[8], whereby graduates are able to offer a very high level of technical skills but lack appropriate work experience and the range of 'soft skills' required by employers in these fields.

Mechanical engineering
Of the 3,815 respondents to the DLHE survey, 74.7% are engaged in employment, which is a slight drop from 2013/14 graduates at 75.2%. Again, this does not suggest a major change in the labour market for mechanical engineers and there is still a significant shortage of skilled and graduate engineers in this field.

Over 60% of graduates employed in the UK are in related engineering professions including mechanical engineers (27.6%), design and development engineers (15.1%) and other engineering professionals (11.4%). As with other engineering degree disciplines this is not surprising given the vocational nature of the courses.

Further study has not changed significantly from 2013/14 (10.3%), with 10.1% of graduates from 2014/15 going into further study. These are mainly graduates from BEng and BSc programmes or those seeking specialist Masters-level courses that may lead to specific roles. Some of the specialist courses include MSc Drone Technology and PGDip System Engineering for Defence Capability, which reflect the increasing

investment in defence technology and the skilled jobs related to this sector.

Unemployment has continued to rise from 7% in 2013/14 to 7.8% for 2014/15 graduates. Given the shortage of skilled engineers and a healthy investment and growth in sectors relating to mechanical engineering, according to the 'Engineering in Employment' report, this does seem surprising, but again this could be due to a number of factors including graduates being unemployed while seeking employment in an engineering profession or a shortage of chartered engineers rather than graduate engineers.

Salaries
Graduates from engineering disciplines are more likely to be in professional or managerial roles six months after graduation compared to all graduates.

This is reflected in the average salaries earned by engineering graduates in full-time paid work in the UK where civil engineering graduates earn £22,700 to £27,100, mechanical engineering graduates earn £21,800 to £28,100 and electrical and electronic engineering graduates earn, £21,400 to £28,600. The average salary for architecture and building graduates has a broader range from £16,200 to £30,200, perhaps reflecting the lower salaries these graduates earn in entry level jobs while they amass the experience to progress in related careers.

Gender
According to 'Engineering UK 2015: The State of Engineering' there is a significant shortage of skilled professionals entering engineering roles and a particular shortage of women entering these professions. In fact, only 7.3% of respondents to the DLHE survey who studied mechanical engineering were female. According to Vince Cable, in the introduction to the Engineering UK report, 'the continued inequality in the uptake and progression of women into engineering remains a problem. There is no way we can generate the number of scientists and engineers the economy requires without addressing this situation'. He goes on to say, however, that, 'with an increase of 8.5% on the number of female First Degree qualifiers in the past year, there are signs that (the government's) efforts to close the gender gap are starting to have an impact'.

An increasing trend in young women taking A-level maths and physics, noted in the same report, as well as the efforts of organisations such as WISE[9] to encourage more women into STEM subjects, may result in a significant change in these statistics over the coming decade.

What of the future?
The report Working Futures 2012- 2022[10] shows that over this period engineering employers will need to recruit 2.56 million people, 257,000 of whom for new vacancies. Overall, 1.82 million of these workers will need engineering skills. This bodes well for future graduates if they can take advantage of opportunities while at university to embrace early career planning, undertake appropriate work experience and develop the soft skills that are a critical factor in successful recruitment to building and engineering positions. Encouraging more school pupils to embrace higher education study in the STEM subjects and thereafter, careers in engineering is a much more challenging problem[11] but solutions to those problems will inevitably result in changes to future destinations.

See references & resources on page 51

ARCHITECTURE AND BUILDING GRADUATES FROM 2015

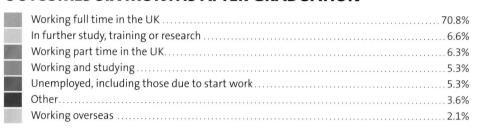

SURVEY RESPONSE: 83.4% | **FEMALE: 1,445** | **MALE: 3,485** | **TOTAL RESPONSES: 4,935** | **ALL GRADUATES: 5,915**

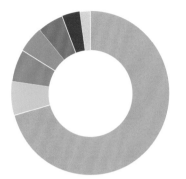

OUTCOMES SIX MONTHS AFTER GRADUATION

Working full time in the UK	70.8%
In further study, training or research	6.6%
Working part time in the UK	6.3%
Working and studying	5.3%
Unemployed, including those due to start work	5.3%
Other	3.6%
Working overseas	2.1%

TYPE OF COURSE FOR THOSE IN FURTHER STUDY

Masters (e.g. MA, MSc) 63.3%

Other postgraduate diplomas 18.1%

Other study, training or research 12.6%

Doctorate (e.g. PhD, DPhil, MPhil) 2.9%

Professional qualification 1.7%

Postgraduate qualification in education 1.5%

Total number of graduates in further study 325

EXAMPLES OF COURSES STUDIED

MBA Executive Facilities Management

MSc City Design and Social Science

BA Graphic Design and Illustration

PGDip Landscape Architecture

Diploma Real Estate Management

TYPE OF WORK FOR THOSE IN EMPLOYMENT

Graduates who were in employment either full time, part time or working and studying in the UK

FEMALE: 1,125 | **MALE: 2,945** | **TOTAL IN EMPLOYMENT IN THE UK: 4,070**

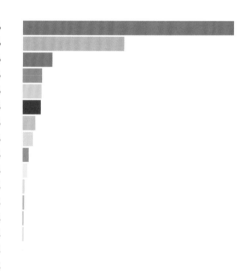

Engineering and building professionals	48.3%
Other professionals, associate professionals and technicians	23.1%
Managers	6.7%
Other occupations	4.4%
Retail, catering, waiting and bar staff	4.3%
Business, HR and finance professionals	4.1%
Marketing, PR and sales professionals	2.9%
Arts, design and media professionals	2.3%
Clerical, secretarial and numerical clerks	1.4%
Legal, social and welfare professionals	1.1%
Education professionals	0.5%
Childcare, health and education occupations	0.4%
Information technology (IT) professionals	0.2%
Unknown occupations	0.2%
Science professionals	0.0%
Health professionals	0.0%

EXAMPLES OF 2015 ARCHITECTURE AND BUILDING GRADUATE JOB TITLES AND EMPLOYERS (SIX MONTHS AFTER GRADUATION)

Construction manager - Bowen Consultants

Case handler - Lloyds Banking Group

Housing officer - UK housing association

Senior design engineer - NGI Consulting

Architect - SDA Architecture Ltd

Landscape architecture - local authority in England

Quantity surveyor - Laing O'Rourke

Events manager - Premier Inn

Exhibition designer - specialist design company

Inspection manager - NHBC

CAD technician - small building services company

Lab technician - Thatchers Cider

Shelf stacker - ASDA

CIVIL ENGINEERING GRADUATES FROM 2015

SURVEY RESPONSE: 82.5% | **FEMALE: 320** | **MALE: 2,005** | **TOTAL RESPONSES: 2,325** | **ALL GRADUATES: 2,820**

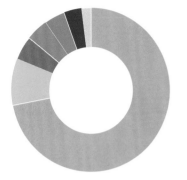

OUTCOMES SIX MONTHS AFTER GRADUATION

Working full time in the UK	72.2%
In further study, training or research	9.1%
Unemployed, including those due to start work	4.8%
Working part time in the UK	4.5%
Working and studying	4.0%
Other	3.7%
Working overseas	1.8%

TYPE OF COURSE FOR THOSE IN FURTHER STUDY

Masters (e.g. MA, MSc) 80.7%

Doctorate (e.g. PhD, DPhil, MPhil) 8.4%

Other study, training or research 4.7%

Other postgraduate diplomas 3.8%

Postgraduate qualification in education 1.9%

Professional qualification 0.5%

Total number of graduates in further study 210

EXAMPLES OF COURSES STUDIED

MSc Project Management

MSc Structural Engineering

MSc Civil Engineering

MRes Geoenvironmental Engineering

BSc Music Production

ACA (Chartered Accountancy)

TYPE OF WORK FOR THOSE IN EMPLOYMENT

Graduates who were in employment either full time, part time or working and studying in the UK

FEMALE: 265 | **MALE: 1,605** | **TOTAL IN EMPLOYMENT IN THE UK: 1,870**

Engineering and building professionals	75.2%	
Other professionals, associate professionals and technicians	4.9%	
Business, HR and finance professionals	3.9%	
Retail, catering, waiting and bar staff	3.8%	
Managers	3.7%	
Other occupations	3.2%	
Clerical, secretarial and numerical clerk occupations	1.4%	
Information technology (IT) professionals	1.0%	
Marketing, PR and sales professionals	0.9%	
Arts, design and media professionals	0.7%	
Education professionals	0.4%	
Legal, social and welfare professionals	0.4%	
Childcare, health and education occupations	0.3%	
Science professionals	0.1%	
Unknown occupations	0.1%	
Health professionals	0.0%	

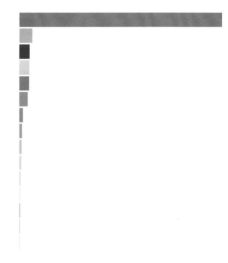

EXAMPLES OF 2015 CIVIL ENGINEERING GRADUATE JOB TITLES AND EMPLOYERS (SIX MONTHS AFTER GRADUATION)

CSD analyst - Credit Suisse

Graduate modeller - Mouchel Consulting

Investment bank analyst - Goldman Sachs

ESSO territory manager - Exxonmobil

Fundraiser - Cancer Research

Orchestra manager - orchestra company

Credit administrator - SMBC

Graduate water engineer - CH2M

ELECTRICAL AND ELECTRONIC ENGINEERING GRADUATES FROM 2015

SURVEY RESPONSE: 81.2% | **FEMALE: 220** | **MALE: 2,065** | **TOTAL RESPONSES: 2,285** | **ALL GRADUATES: 2,815**

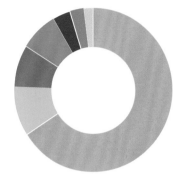

OUTCOMES SIX MONTHS AFTER GRADUATION

Working full time in the UK 66.1%
In further study, training or research 9.7%
Unemployed, including those due to start work 8.3%
Working part time in the UK... 7.8%
Other 3.6%
Working and studying 2.7%
Working overseas 1.8%

TYPE OF COURSE FOR THOSE IN FURTHER STUDY

Masters (e.g. MA, MSc) 48.7%
Doctorate (e.g. PhD, DPhil, MPhil) 35.1%
Other study, training or research 9.4%
Postgraduate qualification in education 3.6%
Other postgraduate diplomas 2.3%
Professional qualification 0.9%
Total number of graduates in further study 220

EXAMPLES OF COURSES STUDIED

MSc Information Security and Digital Forensics
MSc Electrical Engineering
MSc UAV Application and technology

MSc Robotics
MA International Business

TYPE OF WORK FOR THOSE IN EMPLOYMENT

Graduates who were in employment either full time, part time or working and studying in the UK

FEMALE: 165 | **MALE: 1,585** | **TOTAL IN EMPLOYMENT IN THE UK 1,750**

Engineering and building professionals.. 41.2%
Information technology (IT) professionals.. 18.8%
Other professionals, associate professionals and technicians.............. 8.1%
Retail, catering, waiting and bar staff.. 6.8%
Other occupations.. 6.6%
Arts, design and media professionals.. 5.9%
Business, HR and finance professionals 3.5%
Managers 3.0%
Marketing, PR and sales professionals.. 1.9%
Clerical, secretarial and numerical clerk occupations........................ 1.7%
Education professionals 1.2%
Childcare, health and education occupations................................... 0.7%
Legal, social and welfare professionals 0.3%
Science professionals.. 0.2%
Health professionals 0.2%
Unknown occupations.. 0.1%

EXAMPLES OF 2015 ELECTRICAL AND ELECTRONIC ENGINEERING GRADUATE JOB TITLES AND EMPLOYERS (SIX MONTHS AFTER GRADUATION)

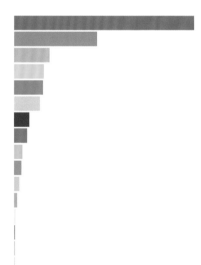

Further education lecturer - educational recruitment agency
Maths tutor - First Class Tutoring
Space systems research associate - UK higher education institution

Design engineer - Bosch
Warhead electronic engineer - specialist engineering company
Software developer - Capita
Insurance broker - Wordell Markell

Translator - small translation company
Customer safety advisor - Sia Security
Technical support engineer - Apple
Sales assistant - small retail company
Warehouse worker - Alliance Healthcare

MECHANICAL ENGINEERING GRADUATES FROM 2015

SURVEY RESPONSE: 83.4% | **FEMALE: 280** | **MALE: 3,535** | **TOTAL RESPONSES: 3,815** | **ALL GRADUATES: 4,575**

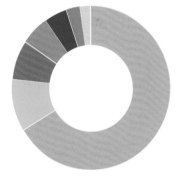

OUTCOMES SIX MONTHS AFTER GRADUATION

Working full time in the UK	66.6%
In further study, training or research	10.1%
Unemployed, including those due to start work	7.8%
Working part time in the UK	6.0%
Other	4.7%
Working and studying	2.7%
Working overseas	2.1%

TYPE OF COURSE FOR THOSE IN FURTHER STUDY

Masters (e.g. MA, MSc) 60.3%
Doctorate (e.g. PhD, DPhil, MPhil) 26.5%
Other study, training or research 7.2%
Postgraduate qualification in education 3.9%
Professional qualification 1.3%
Other postgraduate diplomas 0.9%
Total number of graduates in further study 385

EXAMPLES OF COURSES STUDIED

MSc Finance
MSc Advanced Aeronautical
Engineering
MSc Aircraft Engineering
MSc Drone Technology
PhD Rapid Solidification
PGCE Maths

PGDip in Education and Training
MPDS Chartered Engineer

TYPE OF WORK FOR THOSE IN EMPLOYMENT

Graduates who were in employment either full time, part time or working and studying in the UK

FEMALE: 205 | **MALE: 2,665** | **TOTAL IN EMPLOYMENT IN THE UK: 2,865**

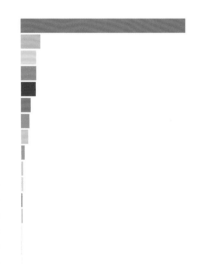

Engineering and building professionals	61.2%
Other professionals, associate professionals and technicians	7.9%
Retail, catering, waiting and bar staff	5.8%
Other occupations	5.8%
Business, HR and finance professionals	5.6%
Managers	3.7%
Information technology (IT) professionals	3.2%
Marketing, PR and sales professionals	2.7%
Clerical, secretarial and numerical clerk occupations	1.3%
Education professionals	0.8%
Arts, design and media professionals	0.8%
Science professionals	0.4%
Childcare, health and education occupations	0.4%
Legal, social and welfare professionals	0.3%
Health professionals	0.1%
Unknown occupations	0.1%

EXAMPLES OF 2015 MECHANICAL ENGINEERING GRADUATE JOB TITLES AND EMPLOYERS (SIX MONTHS AFTER GRADUATION)

Officer cadet - British Army
Design and release engineer - Ford Motor Company
Nuclear electrical control and implementation engineer - Nuvia Ltd
Wind turbine technician - Dong Energy
Graduate global operations - manufacturing company
Reliability engineer - manufacturing company

Trainee accountant - Deloitte LLP
Recruitment consultant - small recruitment company
Prototype buyer - Delphi Diesel Systems
Graphic designer - small design company
City research officer - UK higher education institution
Trainee patent attorney - Keltie LLP

Reliability audit intern - car company
Barista - Costa Coffee
Calibration technician - Bentley

SOCIAL SCIENCE OVERVIEW

WRITTEN BY KIRSTY PALMER

According to the Economic and Social Research Council, 'social scientists influence our lives usually without us being aware they are doing so'[1]. The Campaign for Social Science cites the European Science Foundation, saying 'the social sciences examine what it means to be a social being, ranging from the minutiae of human behaviour and brain functions, to large scale social movements, demographics, economics and politics'[2]. With such wide-ranging definitions, it is no surprise that social science graduates are in demand across a variety of sectors and industries. For example, the well-trodden path of economics graduates going into the financial sector is a justifiable cliché, the 42.8% of graduates from that discipline not working in finance or business are spread evenly across all other sectors.

Analysis of recent outcomes reveals that psychology graduates are entering the police, economists are working in international development and geographers are training to be accountants. The transferable skills developed through the social sciences open many doors for students, so why do graduates from these programmes sometimes struggle to match the attainment of their peers from other degree areas?

There is no doubt that some of the 'traditional' career paths for social scientists have come under pressure in recent years. For example, recruitment in the public sector is at lower levels than previously due to the implementation of austerity measures. However there is some evidence of hard-to-fill vacancies in certain key areas[3], suggesting that if graduates articulate their skills and experience effectively opportunities do still exist within the public sector.

Recent research from the Association of Graduate Recruiters (AGR)[4] also suggests that female graduates are less inclined to apply for graduate schemes than their male colleagues, despite being more likely to succeed when they do. Given that women make up almost two-thirds of all social science graduates, this systemic issue may be hitting them particularly hard. However, employers are aware of this challenge and the same AGR study also reveals that a number of large recruiters are proactively taking steps to attract more female applicants. Women studying social sciences would be well-advised to consider careers in industries that might not otherwise cross their minds, in order to take advantage of these initiatives.

Teaching has long been a popular route for social science graduates, especially those who studied geography, sociology and psychology. However, this year's results see a significant drop across all three disciplines in the proportion of graduates going on to study a PGCE. There can be little doubt that financial concerns play some part in this decline, with more students who are interested in teaching opting to take a direct approach through programmes such as Teach First, now the largest single recruiter of graduates in the country. Their success can be attributed to a combination of factors, including the attractive package available to their teachers and their clever, values-driven marketing and recruitment campaign[5]. Other recruiters seeking to attract social science graduates would be well-advised to centre their ethics around those of their desired candidates, which will help them reach out to a millennial generation who, according to recent research from Deloitte[6], are keen to make a positive impact on the world.

This year's results

Just over thirty-five thousand social science graduates responded to the 2015 Destinations of Leavers from Higher Education (DLHE) survey. Although this is a smaller cohort than the previous year, outcomes remain steady with the majority of graduates in work or study, or some combination of both. Unemployment for social science graduates ranges from 4.9% for geography graduates to 7.6% for sociology graduates.

Economics

Economics graduates remain heavily in demand in the labour market, especially in financial and business roles. They are also significantly less likely to be working in retail, catering, waiting or bar staff roles (6.1%) compared with the wider graduate population working in the UK (11.1%) which means that economics remains one of the subject pathways most likely to immediately result in professional level employment.

Despite the ongoing success of economics graduates in the labour market, a Quality Assurance Agency (QAA) steering group, made up of academic and professional economists, has recommended changes to the undergraduate economics curriculum to ensure that graduates are developing the necessary skills for the future economy. The recommendations were adopted by the QAA in July 2015 and will begin to have an impact on studies over the coming years. This innovation, combined with the traditional strength of economics degrees in the labour market, means that current and prospective students should feel confident about choosing this pathway.

Geography

The Royal Geographical Society is clear that geography graduates can bring a range of skills to a variety of industries. The outcomes for geographers in the 2014/15 DLHE survey reflect this clearly as they are less likely than any other social science graduates to be unemployed (4.9%). Similarly to 2014 there is no specific sector that dominates job outcomes for geography graduates, although they are significantly more likely to be in further study than the wider graduate population (19.4% compared to 13.1%). The nature of postgraduate courses being undertaken, such as Masters and postgraduate qualifications in education, suggests that graduates are seeking to develop specialist skills to prepare them for particular pathways. However, as previously mentioned, the traditional route into teaching seems to be under some threat, with a significant decline in the proportion of postgraduates taking PGCE studies versus the previous year (19.9% in 2014/15 compared with 26.1% in 2013/14).

Law

In a continuing trend from recent DLHE surveys, only roughly one in three law graduates are working in legal or social welfare professions (32.3%), with the remainder spread across a range of occupations. Law graduates are more than twice as likely to be undertaking further study (28.2%) than the rest of the graduate population (13.1%) and, reflecting the demand for the Legal Practice Certificate or Bar Professional Qualification, a much higher proportion of law graduates in further study are undertaking professional qualifications (34.7%) than in the wider graduate population (4.6%).

According to the Law Society 61% of newly-registered solicitors in July 2015 were women[7]. This is in some way refelective of the proportion of female law graduates (64%). Traditionally men have dominated this sector and still represent the majority of solicitors in the UK (51.8% vs. 48.2%). The fastest growing area for solicitor jobs is in in-house legal services rather than more traditional practice-based roles. This means that careers services and other providers of advice for students and graduates must provide information about these pathways.

Politics
Almost one in five politics graduates are in further study following the completion of their degree in 2015, well above the average for all subjects (13.1%). Three-quarters of those studying are undertaking a Masters, often in more specialised areas of politics, including international relations and international human rights, which suggests a clear need for more specific academic expertise in some sectors.

Of those students who are working in the UK, almost one in four (23%) are in business, HR and finance professions compared with 20.8% from 2013/14. Similarly, the proportion of graduates going into retail, catering, waiting and bar staff roles fell to 13.1%. This suggests that politics graduates in particular have been beneficiaries of the increase in graduate recruitment in the last year[8].

Psychology
Psychology remains a popular pathway for students (13,835 students in 2014/15) with psychology graduates representing almost one-third of social science graduates. Overall outcomes are fairly similar to those from the 2014 psychology graduate cohort, however, there has been a marginal drop in the rates of unemployment (5.6% in 2015 compared to 6.2% in 2014) for psychology graduates, which should offer encouragement for current and prospective students.

Overall, psychology graduates are more likely to be working part time in the UK or combining work and study than the wider graduate population, 25.1% compared to 18%. This is perhaps connected to the occupations that employ the largest proportion of psychology graduates, specifically retail, catering or bar work, and childcare, health and education, which both offer a range of part-time opportunities for graduates.

Further study remains a popular choice for psychology graduates completing their first degree (16.2%). It is likely that this is partly down to the need to complete further study in order to enter clinical pathways. Psychology graduates are the most likely of the social science graduates to be undertaking research-led study, with 6.4% of those studying choosing to pursue a Doctorate, although this is still a much lower proportion than the wider graduate population (12.0%).

Challenges around funding and support for research-led study in the social sciences may be at the root of this issue. It was highlighted by the Campaign for Social Sciences, in their 'The Business of People' report[9], that there is a need for increased investment in social science research and postgraduate study in order to reflect the impact it has on the UK economy.

Sociology
2015 sees a small drop in full-time work in the UK for sociology graduates compared with last year (48.4% compared to 50.6%). There has been an increase in sociology graduates from the 2014/15 cohort entering further study (14%) compared to 2013/14 sociology graduates (11.4%), which perhaps reflects the need to develop more specialist skills before entering the labour market. This is further evidenced by the proportion of students undertaking a Masters level course (59.4% of those studying), which has also increased against last year's outcomes.

Around one in ten sociology graduates are working in legal, social and welfare professions with a further 10.6% working in childcare, health and education occupations, presumably because of the experience required to enter into social and welfare professions.

Sociologists are also more likely to be unemployed than the wider graduate population (7.6% compared to 5.7%). There is no doubt that sociology graduates have valuable skills that would benefit employers in a range of roles. The challenge lies in helping students and graduates to understand and articulate those skills, and to seek out relevant work experience while studying in order to develop them.

Conclusion
The labour market welcomes social scientists of all kinds due to their range of skills, empathy with the world and ability to analyse critically. This needs to be matched with confidence from students and graduates to reach out and apply for the widest range of vacancies. As traditional routes for social scientists are narrowed, the need to consider wider options becomes more pressing. However students should take confidence from the engagement of the government with universities and higher education bodies, including the Campaign for Social Science, which is pushing forward the public agenda to ensure that these graduates' skills and contributions will be properly recognised and valued by employers. As long as society exists those people who can understand, interpret and explain it will be crucial to its effective functioning. Social scientists – hold your heads high.

See references & resources on page 51

ECONOMICS GRADUATES FROM 2015

SURVEY RESPONSE: 81.4% | **FEMALE: 1,270** | **MALE: 3,190** | **TOTAL RESPONSES: 4,460** | **ALL GRADUATES: 5,475**

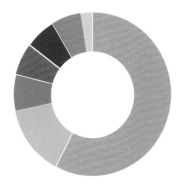

OUTCOMES SIX MONTHS AFTER GRADUATION

Working full time in the UK	57.9%
In further study, training or research	13.8%
Working and studying	7.4%
Unemployed, including those due to start work	6.3%
Other	6.2%
Working part time in the UK	6.1%
Working overseas	2.3%

TYPE OF COURSE FOR THOSE IN FURTHER STUDY

Masters (e.g. MA, MSc) 81.7%

Other study, training or research 6.1%

Doctorate (e.g. PhD, DPhil, MPhil) 4.7%

Other postgraduate diplomas 2.8%

Professional qualification 2.6%

Postgraduate qualification in education 1.9%

Total number of graduates in further study 615

EXAMPLES OF COURSES STUDIED

MSc Finance

MSc Technology and Innovation Management

MSc Economics

MSc Wealth and Investment Management

MSc Economics and Econometrics

MA Consumer Behaviour

PGCE Secondary Maths

Legal Practice Certificate

ACCA (Association of Chartered Certified Accountants)

CIMA (Chartered Institute of Management Accountants)

TYPE OF WORK FOR THOSE IN EMPLOYMENT

Graduates who were in employment either full time, part time or working and studying in the UK

FEMALE: 935 | **MALE: 2,240** | **TOTAL IN EMPLOYMENT IN THE UK: 3,175**

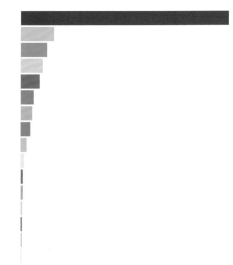

Business, HR and finance professionals	57.2%
Marketing, PR and sales professionals	9.2%
Clerical, secretarial and numerical clerk occupations	7.3%
Retail, catering, waiting and bar staff	6.1%
Managers	5.3%
Other occupations	3.6%
Other professionals, associate professionals and technicians	3.2%
Information technology (IT) professionals	2.7%
Education professionals	1.7%
Legal, social and welfare professionals	1.0%
Engineering and building professionals	0.6%
Childcare, health and education occupations	0.6%
Arts, design and media professionals	0.5%
Science professionals	0.4%
Unknown occupations	0.3%
Health professionals	0.1%

EXAMPLES OF 2015 ECONOMICS GRADUATE JOB TITLES AND EMPLOYERS (SIX MONTHS AFTER GRADUATION)

Maths teacher - secondary school

Software analyst - financial advice provider

Trainee accountant - accountancy firm

Finance analyst - financial services provider

Auditor - KPMG

Finance graduate - Thales Construction

Assistant economist - HM Treasury

Investment banker - Goldman Sachs

Data analyst - media group

Conference organiser - professional body

Buyer - Tesco

Professional footballer

Policy officer - Civil Service

GEOGRAPHY GRADUATES FROM 2015

SURVEY RESPONSE: 81.8% | **FEMALE: 1,175** | **MALE: 855** | **TOTAL RESPONSES: 2,030** | **ALL GRADUATES: 2,480**

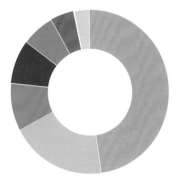

OUTCOMES SIX MONTHS AFTER GRADUATION

Working full time in the UK	48.0%
In further study, training or research	19.4%
Working part time in the UK	9.5%
Other	8.5%
Working and studying	6.6%
Unemployed, including those due to start work	4.9%
Working overseas	3.1%

TYPE OF COURSE FOR THOSE IN FURTHER STUDY

Masters (e.g. MA, MSc) 64.7%
Postgraduate qualification in education 19.9%
Other postgraduate diplomas 7.7%
Doctorate (e.g. PhD, DPhil, MPhil) 3.0%
Other study, training or research 2.7%
Professional qualification 1.9%
Total number of graduates in further study 395

EXAMPLES OF COURSES STUDIED

MSc Meteorology
MSc Applied Ecology
MSc Real Estate Management
MSc Cartography
MSc Anthropology
MA Environment Policy and
Development

PhD Geography and Political
Science
PGCE Secondary

TYPE OF WORK FOR THOSE IN EMPLOYMENT

Graduates who were in employment either full time, part time or working and studying in the UK

FEMALE: 765 | **MALE: 530** | **TOTAL IN EMPLOYMENT IN THE UK: 1,295**

Business, HR and finance professionals	19.5%
Marketing, PR and sales professionals	15.4%
Retail, catering, waiting and bar staff	15.2%
Clerical, secretarial and numerical clerk occupations	8.9%
Education professionals	6.6%
Other professionals, associate professionals and technicians	6.6%
Managers	6.5%
Engineering and building professionals	6.0%
Other occupations	5.9%
Childcare, health and education occupations	3.4%
Legal, social and welfare professionals	2.9%
Information technology (IT) professionals	1.4%
Arts, design and media professionals	1.0%
Science professionals	0.4%
Health professionals	0.2%
Unknown occupations	0.1%

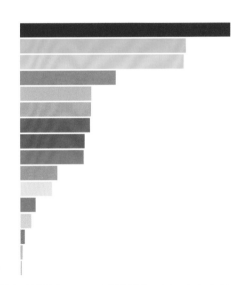

EXAMPLES OF 2015 GEOGRAPHY GRADUATE JOB TITLES AND EMPLOYERS (SIX MONTHS AFTER GRADUATION)

General manager - Network Rail
Management trainee - L'Oréal
Teacher - secondary school
Campaign coordinator - climate change charity
Hydrometry and telemetry officer - Environment Agency
Transport planner - transport planning association

Web developer - charity
Recruitment consultant - recruitment agency
Trainee accountant - accountancy firm
Human resources analyst - JP Morgan
Odds compiler - online gambling company
Trainee catastrophe modeller - insurance underwriter

Buyer - cleaning products manufacturer
Hockey coach - private school
Trainee pilot - Qatar Airways
Social researcher - HM Government
Logistics coordinator - accommodation provider

LAW GRADUATES FROM 2015

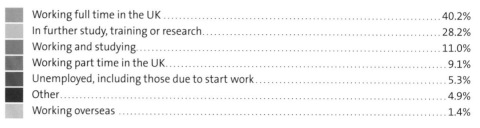

SURVEY RESPONSE: 76.9% | **FEMALE: 6,055** | **MALE: 3,355** | **TOTAL RESPONSES: 9,415** | **ALL GRADUATES: 12,235**

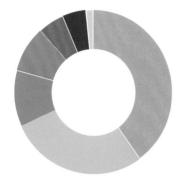

OUTCOMES SIX MONTHS AFTER GRADUATION

Working full time in the UK 40.2%
In further study, training or research 28.2%
Working and studying 11.0%
Working part time in the UK 9.1%
Unemployed, including those due to start work 5.3%
Other 4.9%
Working overseas 1.4%

TYPE OF COURSE FOR THOSE IN FURTHER STUDY

Masters (e.g. MA, MSc) 36.9%
Professional qualification 34.7%
Other postgraduate diplomas 18.5%
Other study, training or research 7.2%
Postgraduate qualification in education 1.8%
Doctorate (e.g. PhD, DPhil, MPhil) 0.8%
Total number of graduates in further study 2,650

EXAMPLES OF COURSES STUDIED

MSc Management
MA Criminal Law and Criminal Justice
LLM International Human Rights
LLM International Comparative and Commercial Law

LLM International Commercial Law
LLM Law
Legal Practice Course
Bar Professional Training Course

TYPE OF WORK FOR THOSE IN EMPLOYMENT

Graduates who were in employment either full time, part time or working and studying in the UK

FEMALE: 3,730 | **MALE: 1,930** | **TOTAL IN EMPLOYMENT IN THE UK: 5,660**

Legal, social and welfare professionals 32.3%
Retail, catering, waiting and bar staff 14.3%
Clerical, secretarial and numerical clerk occupations 13.5%
Business, HR and finance professionals 12.1%
Other occupations 7.4%
Marketing, PR and sales professionals 4.9%
Other professionals, associate professionals and technicians 4.5%
Managers 3.8%
Childcare, health and education occupations 2.3%
Education professionals 1.6%
Information technology (IT) professionals 1.2%
Arts, design and media professionals 1.0%
Health professionals 0.4%
Science professionals 0.3%
Engineering and building professionals 0.3%
Unknown occupations 0.3%

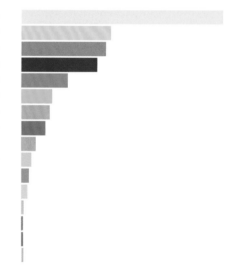

EXAMPLES OF 2015 LAW GRADUATE JOB TITLES AND EMPLOYERS (SIX MONTHS AFTER GRADUATION)

Retail manager - ice cream maker
Service delivery manager - Citizens Advice
Teacher - Teach First

Paralegal - law firm
Trainee solicitor - law firm
Trainee probation officer - National Offender Management Service
Recruitment consultant - recruitment agency

Lettings negotiator - estate agent
Immigration services officer - law firm
Civil Service fast streamer - Civil Service
Operations graduate - Royal Mail
Graduate trainee - John Lewis

POLITICS GRADUATES FROM 2015

SURVEY RESPONSE: 77.4% | **FEMALE: 1,730** | **MALE: 2,310** | **TOTAL RESPONSES: 4,045** | **ALL GRADUATES: 5,225**

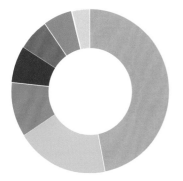

OUTCOMES SIX MONTHS AFTER GRADUATION

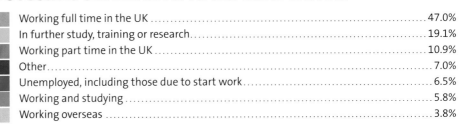

Working full time in the UK	47.0%
In further study, training or research	19.1%
Working part time in the UK	10.9%
Other	7.0%
Unemployed, including those due to start work	6.5%
Working and studying	5.8%
Working overseas	3.8%

TYPE OF COURSE FOR THOSE IN FURTHER STUDY

Masters (e.g. MA, MSc) 75.1%
Other postgraduate diplomas 7.4%
Postgraduate qualification in education 6.2%
Other study, training or research 4.6%
Professional qualification 3.8%
Doctorate (e.g. PhD, DPhil, MPhil) 2.9%
Total number of graduates in further study 770

EXAMPLES OF COURSES STUDIED

MA Human Rights
MA Journalism
MA International Politics
MA Intelligence and Security

MA Conflict, Development and Security
PGCE Primary Education

TYPE OF WORK FOR THOSE IN EMPLOYMENT

Graduates who were in employment either full time, part time or working and studying in the UK

FEMALE: 1,100 | **MALE: 1,470** | **TOTAL IN EMPLOYMENT IN THE UK: 2,570**

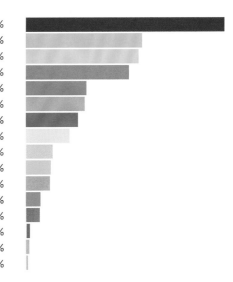

Business, HR and finance professionals	23.0%
Marketing, PR and sales professionals	13.5%
Retail, catering, waiting and bar staff	13.1%
Clerical, secretarial and numerical clerk occupations	12.0%
Other occupations	7.1%
Other professionals, associate professionals and technicians	6.9%
Managers	6.1%
Legal, social and welfare professionals	5.1%
Arts, design and media professionals	3.1%
Education professionals	2.9%
Childcare, health and education occupations	2.8%
Information technology (IT) professionals	1.7%
Science professionals	1.6%
Engineering and building professionals	0.4%
Unknown occupations	0.4%
Health professionals	0.2%

EXAMPLES OF 2015 POLITICS GRADUATE JOB TITLES AND EMPLOYERS (SIX MONTHS AFTER GRADUATION)

Oncology team coordinator - cancer charity
Teacher - Teach First
Volunteer development work - VSO

Recruitment consultant - recruitment firm
Operations graduate - Whitbread
Business analyst - financial services provider
Political consultant - lobbying firm
Marketing assistant - Telegraph Media Group

Graduate trainee - Harper Collins Publishers
Parliamentary researcher - UK Parliament
Regional researcher - police force
Democratic engagement officer - charity

PSYCHOLOGY GRADUATES FROM 2015

SURVEY RESPONSE: 77.1% | **FEMALE: 8,630** | **MALE: 2,035** | **TOTAL RESPONSES: 10,660** | **ALL GRADUATES: 13,835**

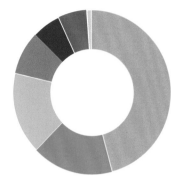

OUTCOMES SIX MONTHS AFTER GRADUATION

Working full time in the UK	46.1%
Working part time in the UK	16.5%
In further study, training or research	16.2%
Working and studying	8.6%
Other	5.9%
Unemployed, including those due to start work	5.6%
Working overseas	1.1%

TYPE OF COURSE FOR THOSE IN FURTHER STUDY

Masters (e.g. MA, MSc) 64.4%
Postgraduate qualification in education 17.7%
Other study, training or research 6.7%
Doctorate (e.g. PhD, DPhil, MPhil) 6.4%
Other postgraduate diplomas 4.3%
Professional qualification 0.5%
Total number of graduates in further study 1,730

EXAMPLES OF COURSES STUDIED

MSc Clinical Psychology
MSc Social Applied Psychology
MSc Mental Health Studies
MSc Forensic Psychology
MSc Health Psychology
MSc Neuroscience
MA Criminal Justice and Criminology

PhD Psychology
PGCE Secondary
PGCE Early Years
NVQ Bakery and Patisserie (Level 2)
ACCA (Association of Chartered Certified Accountants)

TYPE OF WORK FOR THOSE IN EMPLOYMENT

Graduates who were in employment either full time, part time or working and studying in the UK

FEMALE: 6,200 | **MALE: 1,375** | **TOTAL IN EMPLOYMENT IN THE UK: 7,575**

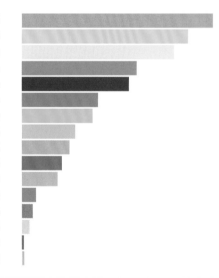

Childcare, health and education occupations	17.5%
Retail, catering, waiting and bar staff	15.2%
Legal, social and welfare professionals	13.9%
Clerical, secretarial and numerical clerk occupations	10.5%
Business, HR and finance professionals	9.8%
Other occupations	7.0%
Marketing, PR and sales professionals	6.5%
Education professionals	4.9%
Other professionals, associate professionals and technicians	4.4%
Managers	3.7%
Health professionals	3.3%
Information technology (IT) professionals	1.3%
Science professionals	1.0%
Arts, design and media professionals	0.7%
Engineering and building professionals	0.2%
Unknown occupations	0.2%

EXAMPLES OF 2015 PSYCHOLOGY GRADUATE JOB TITLES AND EMPLOYERS (SIX MONTHS AFTER GRADUATION)

Retail director - luxury sweet manufacturer
Mental health worker - charity
Social therapist - charity
Retention and attainment officer
Assistant psychologist - NHS
Support worker - mental health charity
Adjudicator - Financial Ombudsman
Paralegal - law firm

Recruitment consultant - recruitment firm
Account manager - food manufacturing
Junior account executive - PR firm
Marketing executive - food manufacturer
Insights analyst - retail analysis firm
Assistant buyer - Tesco
Event coordinator - hotel
Editor/broadcaster - online media platform

Education support worker - secondary school
Special educational needs teaching assistant - primary school
Toy demonstrator - Hamleys

SOCIOLOGY GRADUATES FROM 2015

SURVEY RESPONSE: 75.1% | **FEMALE: 3,960** | **MALE: 1,350** | **TOTAL RESPONSES: 5,315** | **ALL GRADUATES: 7,080**

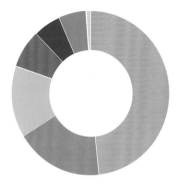

OUTCOMES SIX MONTHS AFTER GRADUATION

Working full time in the UK	48.4%
Working part time in the UK	18.0%
In further study, training or research	14.0%
Unemployed, including those due to start work	7.6%
Other	5.7%
Working and studying	5.3%
Working overseas	1.1%

TYPE OF COURSE FOR THOSE IN FURTHER STUDY

Masters (e.g. MA, MSc) 59.4%
Postgraduate qualification in education 20.7%
Other study, training or research 7.3%
Other postgraduate diplomas 6.9%
Doctorate (e.g. PhD, DPhil, MPhil) 3.5%
Professional qualification 2.2%
Total number of graduates in further study 745

EXAMPLES OF COURSES STUDIED

MA Child and Youth Studies	MSc International Management
MA Social and Public Policy	PGCE Secondary
MA Social Work	PGCE Primary
MA Digital Media	TESOL (Teachers of English to
MA Gender Studies	Speakers of Other Languages)
MSc Town Planning	

TYPE OF WORK FOR THOSE IN EMPLOYMENT

Graduates who were in employment either full time, part time or working and studying in the UK

FEMALE: 2,865 | **MALE: 940** | **TOTAL IN EMPLOYMENT IN THE UK: 3,805**

Retail, catering, waiting and bar staff	20.5%
Clerical, secretarial and numerical clerk occupations	13.5%
Legal, social and welfare professionals	11.5%
Other occupations	11.5%
Childcare, health and education occupations	10.6%
Business, HR and finance professionals	9.6%
Other professionals, associate professionals and technicians	6.7%
Marketing, PR and sales professionals	6.4%
Managers	3.6%
Education professionals	2.7%
Information technology (IT) professionals	1.0%
Health professionals	0.9%
Arts, design and media professionals	0.7%
Science professionals	0.5%
Engineering and building professionals	0.2%
Unknown occupations	0.1%

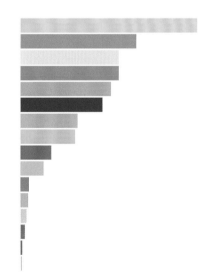

EXAMPLES OF 2015 SOCIOLOGY GRADUATE JOB TITLES AND EMPLOYERS (SIX MONTHS AFTER GRADUATION)

Family practitioner - charity
Teacher - primary school
Teacher - Teach First
Rehabilitation support worker - charity

Recruitment consultant - recruitment agency
Market researcher - market research agency
Fundraising intern - charity
Events manager - church

Police officer - Metropolitan Police
Parliamentary researcher - UK Parliament

ARTS, CREATIVE ARTS AND HUMANITIES OVERVIEW

WRITTEN BY HELEN KEMPSTER

Introduction

The arts, creative arts and humanities encompass a broad range of disciplines. Here we concentrate on fine art, design, performing arts, English, history, media studies and languages, as these are the subject areas with the largest number of graduates. As the subjects in this area are quite varied in their graduate outcomes, we will look at some overall trends before discussing each subject in more detail.

Gender

Females are over-represented in these subject areas, at 63.7% of respondents. Gender differences in subject choices begin at A-level, and to a lesser extent at GCSE. In 2015, art and design subjects, English, drama and French were all amongst the top ten subjects with the biggest gender gaps at A-level[1]. This is possibly due to a number of complex sociological factors such as the stereotypes associated with different subjects and careers, as well as early socialisation. A 2011 Ofsted survey showed that girls hold conventionally stereotypical views about jobs for men and women from an early age[2]. Interestingly, whilst there has been much focus recently on addressing the lack of females studying and working in science, technology, engineering and maths (STEM) subjects, there has been very little converse emphasis on addressing the gender imbalance in the arts and humanities.

Creative arts – fine art, design, performing arts, and media studies

Despite perceptions that the creative industries are difficult for graduates to get started in, the largest proportion of design, media studies and performing arts graduates are working in the UK as arts, design and media professionals. A quarter of fine art graduates also work in this field. This is a buoyant sector; the latest statistics available show that total employment in the creative industries increased by 5.5% between 2013 and 2014, to

1.8 million jobs[3]. However, since career entry into the creative industries is not clearly structured, many graduates can take time to establish themselves. It is also more common for workers to combine multiple roles into a 'portfolio career'[4]. This is reflected in the fact that all of these subjects' graduates, apart from languages, have a higher percentage of graduates working part-time in the UK compared to all graduates (12.9%).

Particularly in their early career, graduates typically take on a variety of roles in service industries to supplement their creative practice and maintain a viable income. These graduates are more likely to be working in retail, catering, waiting and bar staff, compared to 11.1% of all graduates.

Arts and humanities – English, history and languages

Whilst the creative arts subjects are linked to the creative industries, there are fewer clear vocational links between the arts and humanities and the labour market. The occupations of graduates from these subjects in some ways reflect more 'traditional' graduate roles, with business, HR and finance; marketing, PR and sales; and clerical, secretarial and numerical occupations all represented more strongly than across the cluster as a whole. Graduates from these subjects are not clustered in one particular sector; the highest proportion concentrated in one occupational area are the 17% of languages graduates working in marketing, PR and sales.

Fine art

Of fine art graduate respondents 74.8% are female, meaning that this subject has the largest gender gap of any in this subject cluster, closely followed by English (74.6%). The most common job for fine art graduates is artist (16.4%). Due to high prevalence of 'portfolio careers', as found in a recent (2014) survey of artists by the Paul Hamlyn Foundation[5], 30.9% of fine art graduates are working part time, the highest rate in this subject cluster. Of the fine art graduates that go on to further study, 20.8% are studying for qualifications in education. Teaching, along with art therapy and working for community arts projects, offer more socially- and educationally-focused career options to fine art graduates.

Design

In common with previous years, design graduates have the highest rate of full-time employment in this cluster (59.1%), with 42.9% of graduates working in the UK as arts, design and media professionals. The most common job is graphic designer, with clothing designer, artist, interior designer, product designer and industrial designer all featuring in the top ten occupations. Conversely, design graduates were the least likely of those in this cluster to be in further study (3.8%). This could be linked to high employment rate of these graduates; or it could be that they do not feel the need to enter further study immediately after their first degree as they recognise the range of opportunities available to them in the labour market.

Performing arts

The subjects covered here are music, drama and dance. In common with other creative arts subjects, the largest proportion of performing arts graduates are employed as arts, design and media professionals (29.5%). In terms of specific occupations, performing arts graduates are spread across a very wide range of jobs, probably reflecting the variety of the three disciplines covered. Common jobs include acting and presenting; teaching and education; arts officer; photography; and dance and choreography. Again reflecting the prevalence of portfolio working in the creative arts, these graduates are relatively more likely to be working part-time, with just over a quarter (25.9%) doing so.

Opportunities for those studying performing arts are not limited to performance. For example, many students studying drama also develop skills in other areas of the profession such as set design, stage management, writing, prop making or theatre sound. However, for those who do want to perform, Drama UK research has shown that 86% of working actors have had professional training[6], so degree study stands graduates in good stead.

English

The ten most common jobs for this group shows a wide range of occupations, encompassing marketing, writing, public relations, journalism and education. This is due to the fact that English students develop many transferable skills during their studies, which employers across a wide range of sectors value.

Research by the Higher Education Academy's English Subject Centre shows that the most-valued qualities are motivation and enthusiasm; interpersonal skills; team working; oral and written communication; flexibility and adaptability; initiative and productivity; problem solving; planning and organisation; and managing own development[7].

Just over 20% of English graduates went on to further study, with a further 6.8% combining work and study. This is higher than the rate for all graduates. Of these, 31.8% were studying for a qualification in education. Although English is not currently a priority subject for teacher recruitment, it is a core subject in the National Curriculum and there is strong demand for professionals in this area. In addition, there is currently a teacher recruitment crisis in England, with teacher trainee recruitment targets failing to be met in the four years to 2016[8]. A National Audit Office report also found that vacancy rates in English had risen between 2011 and 2014[9]. These factors may be encouraging English graduates to consider teaching as a profession, as they are aware that there is a demand for their skills and subject knowledge.

History

As in previous years, history graduates are the most likely of those in this subject cluster to pursue further study, with 21.8% doing so (compared to 13.1% of all graduates). This further study may be academic in nature, or more vocational, with training in fields as diverse as law, accountancy, journalism, librarianship, teaching and IT. This shows that the study of history provides a firm basis for further career development.

There is similarly a great variety in the types of occupation pursued, with the ten most common jobs including marketing, human resources, and roles in education (particularly as a teaching assistant). In common with English, history graduates are able to draw on the transferable skills they have developed during their degree, such as communication; analytical skills; the use of IT; and working with others.

Media studies

Almost a quarter (23.2%) of media studies graduates work in the UK as art, design and media professionals, compared to 5.9% of all graduates, which suggests that many are finding work in sectors relevant to their studies. A relatively high proportion (23.2%) of media studies graduates work part-time, which relates to the prevalence of portfolio careers in the media sector. Common roles are in the arts, photography, public relations and graphic design.

Looking at longer-term employment rates for these graduates, 2013 data from the Office for National Statistics showed that of all those with a undergraduate degree, media and information studies graduates had the second-highest employment rate of all subjects, second only to medicine[10].

Languages

As might be expected, a relatively high proportion of languages graduates were working overseas (9.9% compared with 1.8% of all graduates). It is reasonable to assume that a large proportion of those are using their language skills in some capacity. In a European survey of employers' perception of graduate employability, 67% stated that foreign language skills were important when recruiting for their companies[11].

These graduates also had the highest upper limit to the salary range of the subjects within this cluster, at £25,100. Employers may well be prepared to pay a premium to employ these graduates, as fluency in a language is not something that organisation can quickly and easily train new recruits up in themselves. Language skills are valuable to employers across all sectors, with the most common jobs spanning marketing; business and sales; writing and translating; human resources; and teaching and education.

However, HESA data shows that, between 2007/08 and 2013/14, languages was the largest subject area to see a fall in student numbers. These declined by 16%, including 25% and 34% decreases in French and German respectively[12]. People in the UK are also amongst the least likely in Europe to be able to speak any foreign language[13]. Therefore those UK graduates who do have foreign language skills are likely to be in great demand.

Conclusion

Arts, creative arts and humanities subjects provide a foundation for students to go on to a broad range of occupations. In general, those studying creative arts subjects are more likely to find work related to their degree studies, whilst the transferable skills gained from arts and humanities allow graduates to enter a wide range of sectors.

See references & resources on page 52

FINE ARTS GRADUATES FROM 2015

SURVEY RESPONSE: 75.7% | **FEMALE: 1,895** | **MALE: 635** | **TOTAL RESPONSES: 2,535** | **ALL GRADUATES: 3,345**

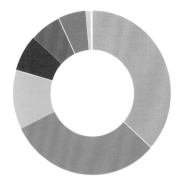

OUTCOMES SIX MONTHS AFTER GRADUATION

Working full time in the UK	36.9%
Working part time in the UK	30.9%
In further study, training and research	11.7%
Other	7.2%
Unemployed, including those due to start work	6.5%
Working and studying	5.5%
Working overseas	1.3%

TYPE OF COURSE FOR THOSE IN FURTHER STUDY

Masters (e.g. MA, MSc) 62.3%

Postgraduate qualification in education 20.8%

Other study, training or research 9.3%

Other postgraduate diplomas 5.3%

Doctorate (e.g. PhD, DPhil, MPhil) 1.4%

Professional qualification 1.0%

Total number of graduates in further study 295

EXAMPLES OF COURSES STUDIED

MA Art and Design

MA Filmmaking

PGCE Secondary Art

NVTQ Catering

City and Guilds Award Education and Training

TYPE OF WORK FOR THOSE IN EMPLOYMENT

Graduates who were in employment either full time, part time or working and studying in the UK

FEMALE: 1,400 | **MALE: 455** | **TOTAL IN EMPLOYMENT IN THE UK: 1,855**

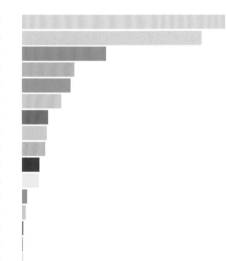

Retail, catering, waiting and bar staff	27.9%
Arts, design and media professionals	24.7%
Other occupations	11.6%
Childcare, health and education occupations	7.2%
Clerical, secretarial and numerical clerks	6.7%
Marketing, PR and sales professionals	5.4%
Managers	3.6%
Education professionals	3.4%
Other professionals, associate professionals and technicians	3.2%
Business, HR and finance professionals	2.4%
Legal, social and welfare professionals	2.3%
Information technology professionals	0.7%
Health professionals	0.5%
Engineering and building professionals	0.2%
Science professionals	0.1%
Unknown occupations	0.1%

EXAMPLES OF 2015 FINE ARTS GRADUATE JOB TITLES AND EMPLOYERS (SIX MONTHS AFTER GRADUATION)

Restaurant manager - catering supplier

Department manager - fashion retailer

Company owner - film production company

Assistant manager - museum

Support worker for adults - mental health charity

Account administrator - marketing agency

Finance officer - nursery

Brand specialist - fashion retailer

Marketing administrator - lettings agency

Video project manager - university

Fine art sales consultant - gallery

Art studio assistant - artist

Designer - toy and game manufacturer

Creative arts officer - dance company

Junior graphic designer - marketing agency

Curatorial assistant - art gallery

Professional athlete

Child support assistant - a primary school

Cover supervisor - secondary school

Nursery school teaching assistant - nursery

Art assistant - middle school

Administration assistant - architects' firm

Account administrator - advertising agency

Forensic case work administrator - forensic services company

DESIGN GRADUATES FROM 2015

SURVEY RESPONSE: 78.7% | **FEMALE: 6,615** | **MALE: 3,165** | **TOTAL RESPONSES: 9,780** | **ALL GRADUATES: 12,435**

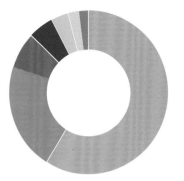

OUTCOMES SIX MONTHS AFTER GRADUATION

Working full time in the UK	59.1%
Working part time in the UK	21.0%
Unemployed, including those due to start work	7.2%
Other	4.9%
In further study, training and research	3.8%
Working overseas	2.2%
Working and studying	1.7%

TYPE OF COURSE FOR THOSE IN FURTHER STUDY

Masters (e.g. MA, MSc) 64.2%

Postgraduate qualification in education 16.9%

Other study, training or research 10.2%

Other postgraduate diplomas 6.0%

Doctorate (e.g. PhD, DPhil, MPhil) 2.0%

Professional qualification 0.7%

Total number of graduates in further study 370

EXAMPLES OF COURSES STUDIED

MA Music Production

MA Surface Pattern and Textiles

MA Games Design

PGCE Lifelong Learning Sector

CIPD Human Resources (Level 3)

TYPE OF WORK FOR THOSE IN EMPLOYMENT

Graduates who were in employment either full time, part time or working and studying in the UK

FEMALE: 5,440 | **MALE: 2,565** | **TOTAL IN EMPLOYMENT IN THE UK: 8,005**

Arts, design and media professionals	42.9%
Retail, catering, waiting and bar staff	18.8%
Marketing, PR and sales professionals	8.8%
Other occupations	8.8%
Clerical, secretarial and numerical clerk occupations	4.9%
Managers	2.9%
Other professionals, associate professionals and technicians	2.8%
Information technology professionals	2.5%
Business, HR and finance professionals	2.1%
Childcare, health and education occupations	1.8%
Engineering and building professionals	1.6%
Education professionals	1.3%
Legal, social and welfare professionals	0.4%
Health professionals	0.2%
Science professionals	0.1%
Unknown occupations	0.1%

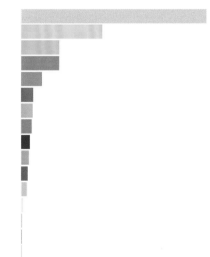

EXAMPLES OF 2015 DESIGN GRADUATE JOB TITLES AND EMPLOYERS (SIX MONTHS AFTER GRADUATION)

Director - creative design studio

Duty manager - stationer

Dental technician - dental laboratory

Sewing tutor - adult day care centre

Community support worker - social enterprise

Research and design engineer - piping manufacturer

Front end web developer - digital agency

Coding specialist - market research company

Recruitment consultant - recruitment agency

Mortgage advisor - Barclays

Digital marketing associate - web agency

Corporate sales executive - food retailer

Fashion buyer - Marks & Spencer

Art director - advertising agency

Copywriter - children's clothes retailer

UX designer trainee - BBC

Product designer - product design consultancy

Self-employed musician

3D artist - computer games company

Trainee costume assistant - television broadcaster

Florist - florist shop

ENGLISH GRADUATES FROM 2015

SURVEY RESPONSE: 77.9% | **FEMALE: 6,420** | **MALE: 2,180** | **TOTAL RESPONSES: 8,600** | **ALL GRADUATES: 11,035**

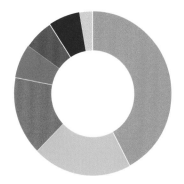

OUTCOMES SIX MONTHS AFTER GRADUATION

Working full time in the UK 42.4%
In further study, training and research.. 20.3%
Working part time in the UK 15.3%
Working and studying 6.8%
Unemployed, including those due to start work 6.2%
Other... 6.2%
Working overseas 2.7%

TYPE OF COURSE FOR THOSE IN FURTHER STUDY

Masters (e.g. MA, MSc) 51.0%
Postgraduate qualification in education 31.8%
Other postgraduate diplomas 5.8%
Other study, training or research 5.1%
Doctorate (e.g. PhD, DPhil, MPhil) 3.6%
Professional qualification 2.7%
Total number of graduates in further study 1,750

EXAMPLES OF COURSES STUDIED

MA Publishing
MA Film, Screen Media and Television
MA Newspaper Journalism
MPhil English Literature
MSc Contemporary Identities

PGCE English
PGCE Primary Teaching
Art Foundation
Graduate Diploma in Law

TYPE OF WORK FOR THOSE IN EMPLOYMENT

Graduates who were in employment either full time, part time or working and studying in the UK

FEMALE: 4,215 | **MALE: 1,320** | **TOTAL IN EMPLOYMENT IN THE UK: 5,540**

Retail, catering, waiting and bar staff 18.7%
Marketing, PR and sales professionals 15.4%
Clerical, secretarial and numerical clerks 13.0%
Arts, design and media professionals.. 9.5%
Education professionals 8.8%
Childcare, health and education occupations................................. 7.9%
Other occupations.. 7.8%
Business, HR and finance professionals 7.6%
Managers 3.3%
Legal, social and welfare professionals 2.8%
Other professionals, associate professionals and technicians 2.6%
Information technology (IT) professionals 1.7%
Health professionals 0.4%
Unknown occupations.. 0.2%
Science professionals... 0.2%
Engineering and building professionals 0.2%

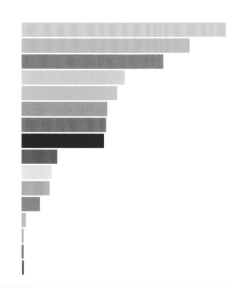

EXAMPLES OF 2015 ENGLISH GRADUATE JOB TITLES AND EMPLOYERS (SIX MONTHS AFTER GRADUATION)

Councillor - local government
Trainee pharmacist - Boots
Early years educator - pre-school
English teacher - secondary school
Regional litigation manager - Civil Service
Legal team member - asset management firm
Charity worker - children's charity
Support worker - mental health charity

Assistant proposal writer - engineering company
Web officer - pub
Informatics analyst - NHS
Research co-ordinator - hospital trust
Investment banker - Morgan Stanley
Marketing and advertising assistant - publisher
Events and hospitality manager - museum

Commissioning editor - media group
Arts management trainee - theatre
Chief reporter - local newspaper
Music management assistant - artist management company
Research assistant in linguistics
Drama assistant

HISTORY GRADUATES FROM 2015

SURVEY RESPONSE: 79.3% | **FEMALE: 4,200** | **MALE: 3,855** | **TOTAL RESPONSES: 8,055** | **ALL GRADUATES: 10,155**

OUTCOMES SIX MONTHS AFTER GRADUATION

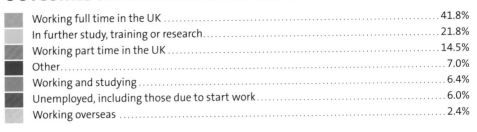

Working full time in the UK	41.8%
In further study, training or research	21.8%
Working part time in the UK	14.5%
Other	7.0%
Working and studying	6.4%
Unemployed, including those due to start work	6.0%
Working overseas	2.4%

TYPE OF COURSE FOR THOSE IN FURTHER STUDY

Masters (e.g. MA, MSc) 59.2%

Postgraduate qualification in education 18.1%

Other postgraduate diplomas 9.6%

Other study, training or research 6.1%

Doctorate (e.g. PhD, DPhil, MPhil) 4.0%

Professional qualification 3.0%

Total number of graduates in further study 1,755

EXAMPLES OF COURSES STUDIED

MA Modern History

MA Fashion Journalism

MA History of Art

MSc International Development

MSc Commercial Building Surveying

MPhil History

Graduate Dipoma in Law

PCGE Secondary

TEFL (Teaching English as a Foreign Language)

Award Leadership and Management (Level 7)

ACA (Chartered accountancy)

TYPE OF WORK FOR THOSE IN EMPLOYMENT

Graduates who were in employment either full time, part time or working and studying in the UK

FEMALE: 2,700 | **MALE: 2,335** | **TOTAL IN EMPLOYMENT IN THE UK: 5,040**

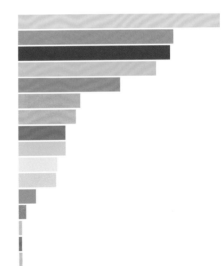

Retail, catering, waiting and bar staff	18.7%
Clerical, secretarial and numerical clerk occupations	14.4%
Business, HR and finance professionals	14.1%
Marketing,.PR and sales professionals	12.8%
Other occupations	9.5%
Childcare, health and education occupations	5.8%
Other professionals, associate professionals and technicians	5.4%
Managers	4.4%
Education professionals	4.4%
Legal, social and welfare professionals	3.6%
Arts, design and media professionals	3.5%
Information technology (IT) professionals	1.6%
Science professionals	0.7%
Health professionals	0.3%
Engineering and building professionals	0.3%
Unknown occupations	0.3%

EXAMPLES OF 2015 HISTORY GRADUATE JOB TITLES AND EMPLOYERS (SIX MONTHS AFTER GRADUATION)

Duty manager - supermarket

Night manager - hotel

Retail manager - coffee shop

Officer cadet - British Army

Rehabilitation support worker - charity

IT support - pet retailer

Executive search consultant - executive search agency

Accountant - Deloitte

Marketing professional - online retailer

Estate agent - estate agency

PR executive - public relations consultancy

Call centre fundraiser - fundraising company

Gallery assistant - museum

Sampler (musician) - record label

Actor - theatre

Tennis coach - fitness club

Personal trainer - gym

Healthcare assistant - NHS

Cover supervisor - secondary school

Teaching assistant - special school

Education assistant - charity

Government caseworker - political party

Partnerships executive - charity

Accounts clerk - an infrastructure services company

MEDIA STUDIES GRADUATES FROM 2015

SURVEY RESPONSE: 75.5% | **FEMALE: 2,010** | **MALE: 1,940** | **TOTAL RESPONSES: 3,945** | **ALL GRADUATES: 5,225**

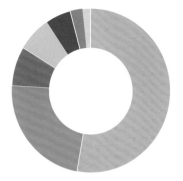

OUTCOMES SIX MONTHS AFTER GRADUATION

Working full time in the UK 52.8%
Working part time in the UK 23.2%
Unemployed, including those due to start work 7.8%
In further study, training or research 6.9%
Other 5.3%
Working and studying 2.5%
Working overseas 1.4%

TYPE OF COURSE FOR THOSE IN FURTHER STUDY
Masters (e.g. MA, MSc) 74.4%
Postgraduate qualification in education 14.3%
Other study, training or research 5.3%
Other postgraduate diplomas 3.1%
Doctorate (e.g. PhD, DPhil, MPhil) 2.4%
Professional qualification 0.6%
Total number of graduates in further study 270

EXAMPLES OF COURSES STUDIED
MA PR and Communications   MA Film Production
MA Publishing   PGCert Academic Practice

TYPE OF WORK FOR THOSE IN EMPLOYMENT
Graduates who were in employment either full time, part time or working and studying in the UK

FEMALE: 1,600 | **MALE: 1,500** | **TOTAL IN EMPLOYMENT IN THE UK: 3,100**

Arts, design and media professionals 23.2%
Retail, catering, waiting and bar staff 22.2%
Marketing, PR and sales professionals 16.2%
Other occupations 11.0%
Clerical, secretarial and numerical clerks 8.9%
Business, HR and finance professionals 4.2%
Information technology (IT) professionals 3.4%
Managers 3.3%
Other professionals, associate professionals and technicians 2.4%
Childcare, health and education occupations 2.3%
Education professionals 1.3%
Legal, social and welfare professionals 1.3%
Engineering and building professionals 0.2%
Unknown occupations 0.1%
Health professionals 0.0%
Science professionals 0.0%

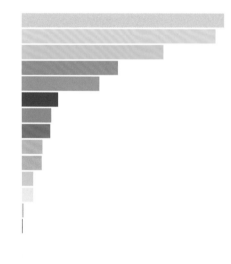

EXAMPLES OF 2015 MEDIA STUDIES GRADUATE JOB TITLES AND EMPLOYERS (SIX MONTHS AFTER GRADUATION)

- Post-16 Manager - secondary school
- English language teacher - language school
- Probate officer - Ministry of Justice
- Creative content manager - marketing agency
- Software tester - software company
- Junior front end developer - advertising agency

- Recruitment consultant - employment agency
- Mortgage advisor - Royal Bank of Scotland
- Insurance underwriter - insurance company
- Account manager - PR company
- Marketing assistant - golf club
- Social media, digital and PR assistant - university
- Copywriter - marketing agency

- Broadcast vision engineer - outside broadcast company
- Bookings casting assistant - television production company
- Blogger - self-employed
- Video journalist - television show
- Trainee assistant director - BBC

LANGUAGES GRADUATES FROM 2015

SURVEY RESPONSE: 78.7% | **FEMALE: 4,885** | **MALE: 2,245** | **TOTAL RESPONSES: 7,135** | **ALL GRADUATES: 9,065**

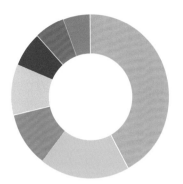

OUTCOMES SIX MONTHS AFTER GRADUATION

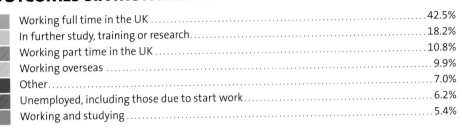

Working full time in the UK	42.5%
In further study, training or research	18.2%
Working part time in the UK	10.8%
Working overseas	9.9%
Other	7.0%
Unemployed, including those due to start work	6.2%
Working and studying	5.4%

TYPE OF COURSE FOR THOSE IN FURTHER STUDY

Masters (e.g. MA, MSc) 49.1%
Postgraduate qualification in education 23.3%
Other postgraduate diplomas 10.0%
Other study, training or research 7.3%
Doctorate (e.g. PhD, DPhil, MPhil) 5.4%
Professional qualification 4.9%
Total number of graduates in further study 1,300

EXAMPLES OF COURSES STUDIED

MA British Sign Language to English Interpretation
MA Shakespeare
MA International Communication and Culture
MSc International Security
HND Civil Engineering

PGCE Secondary Modern Foreign Languages
TEFL (Teaching English as a Foreign Language)
Supporting Teaching and Learning in School (Level 3)
AS Maths

TYPE OF WORK FOR THOSE IN EMPLOYMENT

Graduates who were in employment either full time, part time or working and studying in the UK

FEMALE: 2,910 | **MALE: 1,225** | **TOTAL IN EMPLOYMENT IN THE UK: 4,135**

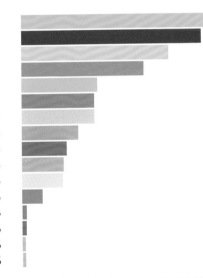

Marketing, PR and sales professionals	17.0%
Business, HR and finance professionals	16.7%
Retail, catering, waiting and bar staff	13.7%
Clerical, secretarial and numerical clerks	11.4%
Education professionals	7.1%
Other occupations	6.8%
Arts, design and media professionals	6.8%
Childcare, health and education occupations	5.3%
Managers	4.2%
Other professionals, associate professionals and technicians	3.9%
Legal, social and welfare professionals	3.8%
Information technology (IT) professionals	1.9%
Science professionals	0.4%
Engineering and building professionals	0.4%
Health professionals	0.3%
Unknown occupations	0.3%

EXAMPLES OF 2015 LANGUAGES GRADUATE JOB TITLES AND EMPLOYERS (SIX MONTHS AFTER GRADUATION)

Manager - charity
Healthcare project manager - NHS
HR manager - language services agency
Area manager - Aldi
Army officer - Army
Science and Spanish supply teacher - secondary school
Pastoral assistant - church
Software support engineer - software company

Field operations associate - Google
HR officer - local authority
Publishing assistant - publisher
Translator - translation agency
Journalist - financial news agency
Operational support officer - police force
International travel consultant - travel agency
German media analyst - market agency

Healthcare assistant - care home
Learning mentor - special school
Language assistant - secondary school
Barista - coffee shop
Waitress - restaurant
Bar staff - restaurant
Security officer - security firm

PERFORMING ARTS GRADUATES FROM 2015

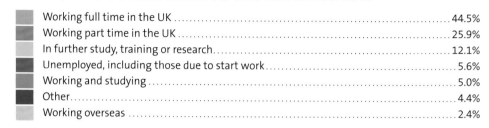

| SURVEY RESPONSE: 77.2% | FEMALE: 4,820 | MALE: 3,495 | TOTAL RESPONSES: 8,320 | ALL GRADUATES: 10,780 |

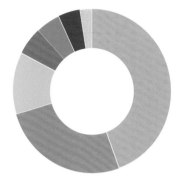

OUTCOMES SIX MONTHS AFTER GRADUATION

Working full time in the UK 44.5%
Working part time in the UK 25.9%
In further study, training or research.. 12.1%
Unemployed, including those due to start work 5.6%
Working and studying 5.0%
Other.. 4.4%
Working overseas 2.4%

TYPE OF COURSE FOR THOSE IN FURTHER STUDY

Masters (e.g. MA, MSc) 46.7%
Postgraduate qualification in education 32.2%
Other study, training or research 10.5%
Other postgraduate diplomas 7.7%
Doctorate (e.g. PhD, DPhil, MPhil) 2.2%
Professional qualification 0.6%
Total number of graduates in further study 1,010

EXAMPLES OF COURSES STUDIED

MA Music Practice
MA Arts Health
MA Theatre Directing
MA Arts and Politics
MA Scriptwriting
MSc Digital and Visual Effects
MSc Real Estate

MMus Instrumental Performance
PGCE Education and Training
PGCE Performing Arts
Sports Massage Therapy
Theatre Making
Screen Acting

TYPE OF WORK FOR THOSE IN EMPLOYMENT

Graduates who were in employment either full time, part time or working and studying in the UK

| FEMALE: 3,640 | MALE: 2,630 | TOTAL IN EMPLOYMENT IN THE UK: 6,270 |

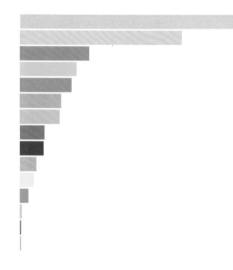

Arts, design and media professionals 29.5%
Retail, catering, waiting and bar staff.. 22.2%
Other occupations... 9.5%
Education professionals 7.8%
Clerical, secretarial and numerical clerk occupations........................... 7.1%
Childcare, health and education occupations..................................... 5.7%
Marketing, PR and sales professionals.. 5.5%
Managers 3.4%
Business, HR and finance professionals 3.3%
Other professionals, associate professionals and technicians................. 2.3%
Legal, social and welfare professionals 2.0%
Information technology professionals... 1.2%
Health professionals 0.3%
Engineering and building professionals 0.2%
Unknown occupations.. 0.2%
Science professionals.. 0.0%

EXAMPLES OF 2015 PERFORMING ARTS GRADUATE JOB TITLES AND EMPLOYERS (SIX MONTHS AFTER GRADUATION)

Manager - pub
Therapy assistant - NHS
Dance teacher - dance school
Music lecturer - university
Maths and English tutor - learning centre
Support worker - local authority
Care worker - social services
Development worker - charity
Assistant engineer - scientific research laboratory

Software developer - web design company
IT consultant - training provider
Web technician - translation company
Associate accountant - Grant Thornton
HR advisor - charity
Artistic director - theatre company
Dance assistant - dance theatre
Graphic designer - signmaker
Choral scholar - cathedral

Assistant care provider - NHS
Teaching assistant - school
Bar staff - pub
Make-up artist - cosmetics company
Lighting technician - theatre
Lifeguard - leisure company
Tour guide - tourist attraction
Carpenter - theatre

BUSINESS AND ADMINISTRATIVE STUDIES OVERVIEW

WRITTEN BY JANE HOWIE

The 2014/15 Destination of Leavers from Higher Education (DLHE survey) indicates that 34,135 or 10.9% of all UK domiciled first-degree graduates studied business and administrative subjects. This is slightly lower than figures from previous years: 11.2% in 2013/14, 11.3% in 2012/13 and 11.4% in 2011/12.

The following provides an analysis of the DLHE data for 2014/15 for the following subject areas:

- finance and accountancy, 7,065 graduates;
- business and management, 18,590 graduates;
- hospitality, leisure, tourism and transport, 4,745 graduates;
- marketing, 3,735 graduates.

Finance and accountancy

Students with accountancy and finance degrees develop a range of subject-specific technical skills including the understanding of accountancy practices and techniques. They also develop transferable skills including numeracy, analytical and problem solving skills[1] which make graduates from accountancy and finance degrees attractive to employers.

Of the graduates who responded to the 2014/15 DLHE survey, 69.3% of finance and accountancy graduates are in employment six months after graduating, 12.2 % are engaged simultaneously with work and further study, and a further 8% engaged with further study only.

Of the 445 finance and accountancy graduates engaged with further study, 13.9% are studying for a professional qualification and 65.8% are engaging in study at Masters level. This trend of engaging with further

study, and the fact it is combined with work, reflects the nature of accountancy and finance related occupations as these often require graduates to undertake further professional qualifications such as ACCA, CIMA or ICAEW.

According to High Fliers research, The Graduate Market in 2016[2]:

- industries or businesses with the largest umber of graduate vacancies for 2016 included: accounting and professional services (4,941 vacancies), investment banking (1,920 vacancies) and banking and Finance (1,509 vacancies);
- PwC and Deloitte, who recruit into accounting and professional services roles, are two of the largest individual recruiters of new graduates in 2016 with 1,540 and 1,100 vacancies respectively.

These trends in graduate vacancies are reflected in the 2014/15 DLHE data which highlights that of the finance and accountancy graduates in employment, 56.8% are employed in professions which are business, HR, and finance related.

Popular roles for those who are employed include: chartered and certified accountants (23.3%); finance and investment analysts (11.3%); and finance and accounting technicians (8.6%).

Commercial awareness is key to success in the finance and accountancy sectors, enabling graduates to show that they can understand the work of a finance organisation as well as that of the companies for which the organisation works.

In addition, we are possibly on the brink of a fourth industrial or technological revolution[3] which is starting to influence the shape of the finance sector, reflected in Association of Chartered Certified Accountants' report 'Professional Accountants – the Future'[4] which states that global connectivity, smart machines and technology are playing a huge role within the sector.

In addition to their accountancy expertise and commercial awareness, employees within the sector must have highly developed professional skills and qualities such as the ability to work collaboratively and influence

others, as well as good technological capabilities.

Business and management

Six months after graduating, 77.1% of the business and management graduates who responded to the 2014/15 DLHE survey are in employment. Popular occupational areas for these graduates include: business, HR and finance (25.1%); marketing, PR and sales (20.8%); and managing (11.4%). Some of the specific job titles they are employed under include: marketing associates (7.5%); business sales executives (3.9%); and finance and investment analysts (3.5%). This data indicates business and management graduates are securing employment related to their degree subject.

Of the business and management graduates who are employed, 11.9% are in clerical, secretarial and numerical clerk occupations. In this instance it can legitimately be argued that these graduates are gaining relevant experience and expanding their professional network in order to make the transition to a professional or managerial role.

According to the report The Graduate Labour Market 2016[5], vacancies in the consultancy sector have increased by 63% since 2006. This is a popular sector which business and management graduates gravitate towards. This sector covers a broad range of consulting, including: strategic consulting; organisational planning; marketing; IT consulting; human resource consulting; and business process management.

It is dominated by the 'Big Four' of Deloitte, EY, KPMG, and PwC. However, due to drivers such as globalisation and the technological revolution, more boutique and niche consulting firms are emerging within the sector. These firms offer organisations specialised consulting services focusing on particular areas of expertise such as logistics, financial transactions or procurement, offering graduates a wider range of employment possibilities.

The salary range for business and management graduates at six months after graduation is: £17,500 to £36,000. According the report The Graduate Labour Market 2016[6], the median starting salary for new graduates joining the UK's leading employers in 2016 is

£30,000. This is based on a survey of the Top 100 companies and what they intend to pay graduates. The median starting salary for the consultancy sector is £31,500.

The salary range for graduates from business and management subjects is wider than the three other business and administrative subject areas, though this could be explained by the location of consultancy roles which tend to be within London. (Please note, the Graduate Labour Market 2016 refers only to The Times Top 100 Graduate Employers where salaries tend to be higher.)

Hospitality, tourism, transport and logistics
According to the 2014/15 DLHE data, 80.4% of the hospitality, leisure, tourism and transport graduates are in employment six months after finishing their degree. Of those in employment in the UK, 37.8% are in either marketing, PR and sales roles (28.6%) or managerial occupations (9.2%) such as conference, exhibition managers and organisers or marketing professionals.

This suggests graduates are securing professional and managerial roles which are linked to their degree subject subjects. A further 27.9% are in occupational areas including clerical, secretarial and numerical clerks (11.5%) and retail, catering, waiting and bar staff roles (16.4%).

According to the Graduate Recruitment Bureau [7] there is an emphasis in this sector upon personal attributes and experience gained through holiday and volunteering work. Employers recruit individuals who have strong interpersonal skills and can motivate and communicate with others since these will play a key part in any position.

This is regardless of whether the recruit is in a customer-facing role or managing colleagues as part of a wider team.

As with business and management graduates, it can be argued that graduates from hospitality, tourism, transport and logistics are gaining experience in entry-level roles in order to enhance their skills set and develop professional networks to make the transition into a professional or managerial role.

With regard to further study, only 4.8% of hospitality, leisure, tourism and transport graduates are engaged with this activity compared to 13.1% of graduates from all subject disciplines.

This is partially reflected in the fact that many roles, particularly within hospitality and tourism, do not require a postgraduate qualification. Instead, there is an emphasis upon undertaking professional qualifications and engaging with professional bodies in order for employees to develop their skillset further and demonstrate their expertise of the sector.

Marketing
In 2014/2015, 10.9% of graduates from business and administrative subjects graduated with a marketing degree. Six months after graduating, 82.5% of all marketing graduates are in employment. This compares positively to the number of graduates from all subjects who are in employment, which is 71.2%.

The DLHE data suggests that marketing graduates are entering roles which are linked to their degrees, with 51.1% of all marketing graduates who are in employment having secured roles in marketing, PR and sales occupations. This figure is nearly seven times higher than the figure for graduates from all subjects who enter into marketing, PR and sales occupations (7.4%).

According to Prospects [8] during their time at university, marketing graduates will have developed their creative thinking and communications skills as well as transferable skills in the areas of: strategic planning and thinking; research, analysis and presentation skills; and using initiative.

The marketing sector is constantly changing, according to the Graduate Recruitment Bureau [9]. Global advances in digital technology means there is now a shift in the skills which marketing recruiters demand from graduates.

Although the ability to generate original ideas and concepts are still sought, the growth in analytical marketing and market intelligence has resulted in the demand for graduates, particularly those from marketing degrees, to have numeracy skills, the ability to solve problems, interpret trends and translate them into strong business cases.

In terms of further study, 3.9% of marketing graduates are engaged with this activity. This is substantially lower than the percentage of graduates from all subjects engaged in further study, which is 13.1%. This may be partly explained by the fact that the marketing sector is extremely competitive

and most employers within the marketing sector may not require any recruits to have formal postgraduate qualifications, instead favouring particular skills, attributes and experience.

See references & resources on page 52

FINANCE AND ACCOUNTANCY GRADUATES FROM 2015

SURVEY RESPONSE: 79.1% | **FEMALE: 2,300** | **MALE: 3,285** | **TOTAL RESPONSES: 5,585** | **ALL GRADUATES: 7,065**

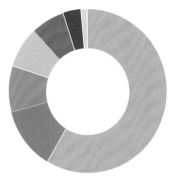

OUTCOMES SIX MONTHS AFTER GRADUATION

Working full time in the UK	58.7%
Working and studying	12.2%
Working part time in the UK	9.3%
In further study, training or research	8.0%
Unemployed, including those due to start work	6.9%
Other	3.6%
Working overseas	1.3%

TYPE OF COURSE FOR THOSE IN FURTHER STUDY

Masters (e.g. MA, MSc) 65.8%
Professional qualification 13.9%
Other study, training or research 8.3%
Other postgraduate diplomas 6.4%
Postgraduate qualification in education 4.7%
Doctorate (e.g. PhD, DPhil, MPhil) 0.9%
Total number of graduates in further study 445

EXAMPLES OF COURSES STUDIED

MSc Financial Mathematics
MSc Accounting and Finance
Graduate Law Diploma
PGCE Primary Teaching
CIPFA (The Chartered Institute of
Public Finance and Accounting)

ACCA (Association of Chartered
Certified Accountants)
CIMA (Chartered Institute of
Management Accountants)

TYPE OF WORK FOR THOSE IN EMPLOYMENT

Graduates who were in employment either full time, part time or working and studying in the UK

FEMALE: 1,845 | **MALE: 2,625** | **TOTAL IN EMPLOYMENT IN THE UK: 4,470**

Business, HR and finance professionals	56.8%
Clerical, secretarial and numerical clerk occupations	17.8%
Retail, catering, waiting and bar staff	7.3%
Other occupations	5.3%
Managers	3.8%
Marketing, PR and sales professionals	3.5%
Other professionals, associate professionals and technicians	1.7%
Information technology (IT) professionals	1.0%
Education professionals	0.7%
Childcare, health and education occupations	0.7%
Legal, social and welfare professionals	0.6%
Engineering and building professionals	0.3%
Arts, design and media professionals	0.3%
Unknown occupations	0.1%
Health professionals	0.1%
Science professionals	0.0%

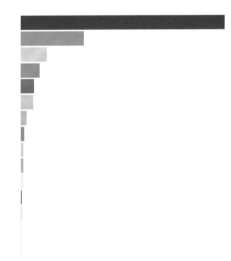

EXAMPLES OF 2015 FINANCE AND ACCOUNTANCY GRADUATE JOB TITLES AND EMPLOYERS (SIX MONTHS AFTER GRADUATION)

Property development manager
Quality surveyor - home building company
Finance graduate - DHL
Financial engineer - credit risk management company
Statutory reporting accountant - British American Tobacco
Graduate accountant - KPMG
Auditor - finance organisation

City research officer - higher education institution
Accounts clerk - upholstery company
Commissions Assistance - private finance company
Accountant - securities company
Account assistant - HMRC
Receptionist
Sales invoice clerk - financial services firm

Waiter - restaurant
Supermarket assistant - Morrisons
Online grocery driver - Sainsbury's
Merchandiser - Monsoon Accessorize

BUSINESS AND MANAGEMENT GRADUATES FROM 2015

SURVEY RESPONSE: 76.6% | **FEMALE: 6,610** | **MALE: 7,620** | **TOTAL RESPONSES: 14,235** | **ALL GRADUATES: 18,590**

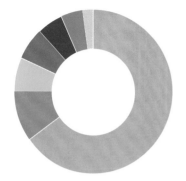

OUTCOMES SIX MONTHS AFTER GRADUATION

Working full time in the UK 65.2%
Working part time in the UK 9.9%
In further study, training or research 6.8%
Unemployed, including those due to start work 6.3%
Other 5.4%
Working and studying 4.4%
Working overseas 2.0%

TYPE OF COURSE FOR THOSE IN FURTHER STUDY

Masters (e.g. MA, MSc) 71.3%
Postgraduate qualification in education 9.9%
Other study, training or research 8.6%
Other postgraduate diplomas 5.3%
Professional qualifications 3.5%
Doctorate (e.g. PhD, DPhil, MPhil) 1.4%
Total number of graduates in further study 965

EXAMPLES OF COURSES STUDIED

MSc Business and Management
MSc Entrepreneurship
MA Management
MBA Quantity Surveying
BSc Quantity Surveying
BA Real Estate Management
PGCE Education

PGCE Further Education
PGCE Secondary Education
ACCA (Association of Chartered Certified Accountants)
NVQ Leadership/ILM (level 5)
Teaching English as a Foreign Language (TEFL)

TYPE OF WORK FOR THOSE IN EMPLOYMENT

Graduates who were in employment either full time, part time or working and studying in the UK

FEMALE: 5,270 | **MALE: 6,035** | **TOTAL IN EMPLOYMENT IN THE UK 11,310**

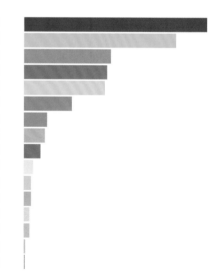

Business, HR and finance professionals 25.1%
Marketing, PR and sales professionals 20.8%
Clerical, secretarial and numerical clerk occupations 11.9%
Managers 11.4%
Retail, catering, waiting and bar staff 11.1%
Other occupations 6.6%
Information technology (IT) professionals 3.2%
Other professionals, associate professionals and technicians .. 2.9%
Engineering and building professionals 2.3%
Legal, social and welfare professionals 1.3%
Education professionals 1.0%
Childcare, health and education occupations 1.0%
Arts, design and media professionals 0.8%
Health professionals 0.3%
Unknown occupations 0.2%
Science professionals 0.1%

EXAMPLES OF 2015 BUSINESS AND MANAGEMENT GRADUATE JOB TITLES AND EMPLOYERS (SIX MONTHS AFTER GRADUATION)

ECommerce manager - natural products company
Operations director - trampoline company
Trading manager - McDonalds
Self-employed beauty salon owner
Teaching English as a Foreign Language (TEFL) teacher - Thailand
Achievement mentor - high school
Volunteer - charitable organisation

Trainee quantity surveyor - construction company
IT sales - data management company
Channel sales specialist - media company
Campaign manager
Procurement graduate - Premier Food
Hospitality coordinator - theatre company
Research assistant - higher education institution

Carer - Allied Healthcare
Transport coordinator
HR administrator - B&Q
Medical secretary - hospital
Supervisor - JD Sports
Station assistant - rail company

HOSPITALITY, LEISURE, TOURISM AND TRANSPORT GRADUATES FROM 2015

SURVEY RESPONSE: 77.3% | **FEMALE: 2,485** | **MALE: 1,180** | **TOTAL RESPONSES: 3,665** | **ALL GRADUATES: 4,745**

OUTCOMES SIX MONTHS AFTER GRADUATION

Working full time in the UK	63.0%
Working part time in the UK	14.4%
Other	6.0%
Unemployed, including those due to start work	6.0%
In further study, training or research	4.8%
Working overseas	3.0%
Working and studying	2.8%

TYPE OF COURSE FOR THOSE IN FURTHER STUDY

Masters (e.g. MA, MSc) 57.5%

Other study, training or research 16.5%

Postgraduate qualification in education 15.3%

Professional qualification 5.4%

Other postgraduate diplomas 3.6%

Doctorate (e.g. PhD, DPhil, MPhil) 1.7%

Total number of graduates in further study 175

EXAMPLES OF COURSES STUDIED

MSc Strength and Conditioning

MSc Accounting

MA Research

BA Exercise and Fitness

PGCE with QTF Trainee Teacher

CPD (Continuing Professional Development) Marketing

TYPE OF WORK FOR THOSE IN EMPLOYMENT

Graduates who were in employment either full time, part time or working and studying in the UK

FEMALE: 2,035 | **MALE: 900** | **TOTAL IN EMPLOYMENT IN THE UK: 2,935**

Marketing, PR and sales professionals	28.6%
Retail, catering, waiting and bar staff	16.4%
Other occupations	14.6%
Clerical, secretarial and numerical clerk occupations	11.5%
Managers	9.2%
Business, HR and finance professionals	8.4%
Other professionals, associate professionals and technicians	5.0%
Childcare, health and education occupations	2.0%
Education professionals	1.2%
Legal, social and welfare professionals	0.9%
Arts, design and media professionals	0.8%
Information technology (IT) professionals	0.6%
Health professionals	0.3%
Science professionals	0.2%
Unknown occupations	0.2%
Engineering and building professionals	0.0%

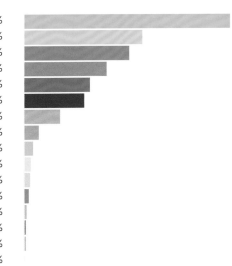

EXAMPLES OF 2015 HOSPITALITY, LEISURE, TOURISM AND TRANSPORT GRADUATE JOB TITLES AND EMPLOYERS (SIX MONTHS AFTER GRADUATION)

Associate product manager - Johnson and Johnson

Sports tutor - college

Self-employed scout analyst - sport trader betting

CV consultant - recruitment agency

PR executive - hotel

Events manager - Capita

Graduate trainee in adventure sports - college

Artillery communications systems signaller - British Army

Personal trainer - hotel gym

Volunteer - outdoor centre

Re-enablement worker - education specialist

PE teaching assistant - school

Office administrator - high street bank

Office administrator - hotel chain

Admin assistant - golf club

Front of house supervisor - bar

Sales assistant - New Look

Experience assistant - hotel

Crane worker - construction

Chalet host - luxury chalet company

MARKETING GRADUATES FROM 2015

SURVEY RESPONSE: 78.8% | **FEMALE: 1,750** | **MALE: 1,190** | **TOTAL RESPONSES: 2,945** | **ALL GRADUATES: 3,735**

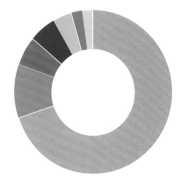

OUTCOMES SIX MONTHS AFTER GRADUATION

Working full time in the UK	69.9%
Working part time in the UK	10.4%
Unemployed, including those due to start work	6.0%
Other	5.6%
In further study, training or research	3.9%
Working and studying	2.1%
Working overseas	2.1%

TYPE OF COURSE FOR THOSE IN FURTHER STUDY
Masters (e.g. MA, MSc) 78.1%
Other study, training or research 8.8%
Postgraduate qualification in education 7.0%
Other postgraduate diplomas 3.5%
Doctorate (e.g. PhD, DPhil, MPhil) 2.6%
Professional qualification 0.0%
Total number of graduates in further study 115

EXAMPLES OF COURSES STUDIED
MA Public Relations and Society   MSc Marketing
MA Advertising and Marketing

TYPE OF WORK FOR THOSE IN EMPLOYMENT
Graduates who were in employment either full time, part time or working and studying in the UK

FEMALE: 1,460 | **MALE: 960** | **TOTAL IN EMPLOYMENT IN THE UK: 2,420**

Marketing, PR and sales professionals	51.1%
Retail, catering, waiting and bar staff	12.6%
Business, HR and finance professionals	8.9%
Clerical, secretarial and numerical clerk occupations	8.4%
Other occupations	5.7%
Managers	5.4%
Arts, design and media professionals	2.3%
Information technology (IT) professionals	1.8%
Other professionals, associate professionals and technicians	1.6%
Childcare, health and education occupations	0.8%
Legal, social and welfare professionals	0.8%
Education professionals	0.4%
Engineering and building professionals	0.2%
Health professionals	0.1%
Unknown occupations	0.1%
Science professionals	0.0%

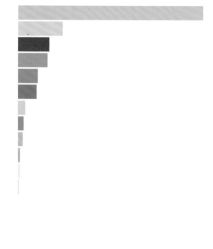

EXAMPLES OF 2015 MARKETING GRADUATE JOB TITLES AND EMPLOYERS (SIX MONTHS AFTER GRADUATION)

Assistant manager - Showcase Cinemas
Director - property development
Marketing volunteer - community organisation
Commercial project manager - furnishing company
Recruitment consultant - recruitment agency

Self-employed marketeer
Loyalty marketing executive - Homebase
Sales specialist - Disneyland
Launchpad graduate - media company
Project executive - events company
Model - modelling agency
Research assistant - media communication company
Merchandiser - Next

Receptionist and intern - communication agency
Store supervisor - Schuh
Customer assistant - Marks & Spencer
Clinique consultant - Clinique, Estée Lauder Company

DATA EXPLAINED – SURVEY RESPONSE

These 'data explained' pages will show you how we have derived our findings from HESA's DLHE data, in the hope that anyone will be able to recreate the figures should they wish.

EACH DATA PAGE IS SPLIT INTO TWO SECTIONS:

1. **Survey response** is at the top of the page and details the outcomes, type of course studied by those in further study, training or research and for each subject data page examples are provided of specific courses that 2014/15 graduates were studying at the time of the survey.
2. **Type of work** – for those in employment in the UK, this details graduates who were employed in the type of work categories, developed by HECSU, as percentages of the total of graduates who were working in the UK. For each subject page examples are provided of specific job titles and employers that 2014/15 graduates were working for at the time of the survey.

OUTCOMES – are based on the activities that graduates who responded said they were doing at the time of the survey

Working full time in the UK
Includes those listing their activity as working full time, including self-employed/freelance, voluntary or other unpaid work, developing a professional portfolio/creative practice or on an internship in the UK

Working part time in the UK
Includes those listing their activity as working part time, including self-employed/freelance, voluntary or other unpaid work, developing a professional portfolio/creative practice or on an internship in the UK

Working overseas
Includes those listing their activity as in full-time or part-time work, including self-employed/freelance, voluntary or other unpaid work, developing a professional portfolio/creative practice or on an internship, overseas

Working and studying
Includes those listing their main activity as working full time or part time and their other activities included full-time or part-time study, training or research and those listing their main activity as in full-time or part-time study, training or research, and their other activities included working full time or part time, in the UK or overseas

In further study, training or research
Includes those listing their activity as either in full-time or part-time study, training or research in the UK or overseas

Unemployed, including those due to start work
Includes those listing their activity as unemployed, and looking for work or those due to start work in the next month

Other
Includes those taking time out in order to travel or doing something else

TYPE OF COURSE FOR THOSE IN FURTHER STUDY – provides a breakdown of the courses studied by graduates who were in further study, training or research, presents the percentages of graduates who were in further study and were studying for a:

Doctorate (e.g. PhD, DPhil, MPhil)
Includes those who were in further study, training or research for a 'Higher degree, mainly by research (e.g. PhD, DPhil, MPhil)'

Masters (e.g. MA, MSc)
Includes those who were in further study, training or research for a 'Higher degree, mainly by taught course (e.g. MA, MSc)'

Postgraduate qualification in education
Includes those who were in further study, training or research for a 'Postgraduate diploma or certificate (including PGCE)' and were studying a subject in education

Other postgraduate diplomas
Includes those who were in further study, training or research for a 'Postgraduate diploma or certificate' but were not studying a subject in education

Professional qualification
Includes those who were in further study, training or research for a 'Professional qualification (e.g. Legal Practice Course, Chartered Institute of Marketing)'

Other study, training or research
Includes those who were in further study, training or research for a 'First degree (e.g. BA, BSc, MEng etc.)', 'Other diploma or certificate', 'Other qualification', 'Not aiming for a formal qualification' or 'Unknown'

PLEASE NOTE – YOU CAN ONLY COMPARE THIS YEAR'S DATA TO THE LAST THREE YEARS' DATA

Due to rounding of percentages to one decimal place on all data pages and first destination tables in subject editorials, the percentages may not equal 100.0% when added together. All numbers used on these pages, where they refer to people, are rounded to the nearest five in accordance with HESA's data reporting requirements.

DATA EXPLAINED – TYPE OF WORK

Respondents to the DLHE survey are asked to give their main job title and a brief description of their role. This information is used to derive their Standard Occupational Classification (SOC 2010 (DLHE)). These SOC 2010 (DLHE) codes are used to calculate the type of work categories used in What do graduates do?. SOC 2010 (DLHE) was only introduced for the 2011/12 survey and cannot be compared with data prior to 2011/12.

The Standard Occupational Classifications 2010 (DLHE) which are under each type of work category are described below.

Managers
Chief executive officers and senior officials/senior officers in protective services/financial institution managers/advertising and marketing directors/managers and directors in transport & logistics, retail & wholesale/managers and proprietors in agriculture, hospitality and leisure, health and care services and other services/property, housing and estate managers/research and development managers/production and functional managers

Health professionals
Medical practitioners/nurses/midwives/paramedics/pharmacists/dental practitioners/ophthalmic opticians/medical radiographers/physiotherapists/occupational or speech and language therapists/podiatrists/other health associate professionals

Education professionals
Teaching professionals in higher education, further, secondary, primary and nursery education and special needs education/senior professionals in educational establishments/education advisers & school inspectors/other educational professionals

Legal, social and welfare professionals
Barristers and judges/solicitors/legal associate professionals/other legal professionals/clinical, education and occupational psychologists/counsellors/probation officers/social workers/youth and community workers/child and early years officers/housing officers/welfare and housing associate professionals/clergy

Science professionals
Chemists/biologists/physicists/physiologists/geophysicists/geologists and meteorologists/social and humanities scientists/bacteriologists, microbiologists/biochemists, medical scientists/other natural and social science professionals

Engineering and building professionals
Civil, mechanical, electrical, electronics engineers/design and development engineers/production and process engineers/architects, town planners and surveyors/construction project managers and related professions

Information technology (IT) professionals
IT specialist managers/IT project and programme managers/IT business analysts, architects and systems designers/programmers and software development professionals/web design and development professionals/IT technicians/other IT and telecommunications professionals

Business, HR and finance professionals
Actuaries, economists & statisticians/management consultants and business analysts/chartered and certified accountants/estimators, valuers and assessors/brokers/insurance underwriters/finance and investment analysts and advisers/taxation experts/financial and accounting managers and technicians/human resources and industrial relations officers/vocational and industrial trainers and instructors

Marketing, PR and sales professionals
Public relations (PR) professionals/buyers and procurement officers/business sales executives/marketing associate professionals/estate agents and auctioneers/sales accounts & business development managers/conference & exhibition managers and organisers

Arts, design and media professionals
Journalists/artists/authors, writers and translators/actors, entertainers and presenters/dancers and choreographers/musicians/arts officers, producers and directors/photographers, audio-visual and broadcasting equipment operators/graphic designers/commercial artists/interior designers/industrial designers/ textile, clothing, furniture and jewellery designers/other design occupations/ clothing advisers, consultants

Other professionals, associate professionals and technicians
Conservation & environment professionals/media and other researchers/ librarians, archivists and curators/quality control and regulatory professionals/ laboratory technicians/science, engineering and production technicians/ draughtspersons and related architectural technicians/protective service occupations/sports and fitness occupations/air craft controllers and aircraft pilot and flight engineers/careers advisers and vocational guidance specialists/public services professionals

Childcare, health and education occupations
Nursery nurses and assistants/childminders/playworkers/teaching assistants/educational support assistants/animal care and control occupations/nursing auxiliaries and assistants/dental nurses/care workers and home carers/other caring personal services

Clerical, secretarial and numerical clerk occupations
National and local government administrators/book-keepers, payroll managers and wages clerks/bank and post-office clerks/other financial administrators/ records clerks and assistants/pensions and insurance clerks and assistants/stock control and transport and distribution clerks and assistants/library clerks and assistants/human resources administrators/sales administrators/office managers/medical, legal and other secretaries/personal assistants/receptionists

Retail, catering, waiting and bar staff
Sales supervisors/sales and retail assistants/retail cashiers and check-out operators/customer service managers and supervisors/kitchen and catering assistants/waiters and waitresses/bar staff/leisure and theme park attendants

Other occupations
Farmers/gardeners & landscapers/groundsmen & greenkeepers/metal machining, fitting and instrument making trades/vehicle trades/electrical and electronic trades/plumbers, carpenters & joiners/bricklayers/ painters and decorators/textile and garment trades/printers/food preparation occupations/catering & bar managers/florists/glass, ceramics & furniture makers/sports and leisure assistants/travel agents/air and rail travel assistants/hairdressers and beauticians/housekeepers/ pharmacy and other dispensing assistants/sales related occupations/merchandisers and window dressers/call and contact centre occupations/market research interviewers/process, plant and machine operatives/assemblers and routine operatives/construction operatives/road transport drivers/other drivers and transport operatives/farm and forestry workers/postal workers and mail sorters/cleaners & domestics/security guards/other elementary occupations

Unknown occupations
Graduates who indicated that they were in employment in the UK but the occupational information provided was inadequate for coding purposes

To see the full list of SOC 2010 (DLHE) codes in each type of work category, go to the What do graduates do? page at www.hecsu.ac.uk

BENEFITS OF AGCAS MEMBERSHIP

Networking opportunities with careers and employability professionals

Professional development via conferences, training, events and level 7 qualifications

Access resources including ARENA and Phoenix

Join AGCAS task groups

REFERENCES & RESOURCES

SCIENCE

1 Department for Business, Innovation & Skills, (May 2015) '2010 to 2015 government policy: public understanding of science and engineering', *www.gov.uk/government/publications/2010-to-2015-government-policy-public-understanding-of-science-and-engineering/2010-to-2015-government-policy-public-understanding-of-science-and-engineering*. **2** H.M. Treasury, Department for Business, Innovation & Skills & the Rt Hon. Greg Clark M.P., (Dec 2014), 'Our Plan for Growth: Science and Innovation', www.gov.uk/government/publications/our-plan-for-growth-science-and-innovation/ *3 Department for Business, Innovation & Skills, (May 2016), 'Wakeham Review of STEM degree provision and graduate employability', www.gov.uk/government/publications/stem-degree-provision-and-graduate-employability-wakeham-review.* **4** Ibid, p16. **5** Ibid, p17. **6** An extra £400 million has been allocated by the government to support research in universities until 2021. Higher Education Funding Council for England, (4 March 2016), 'Funding for higher education in England for 2016-17: HEFCE grant letter from BIS', *www.hefce.ac.uk/news/newsarchive/2016/Name,107598,en.html.* **7** Royal Society for Chemistry, *www.rsc.org*; The Royal Society of Biology, *www.rsb.org.uk*; Institute for Physics, *www.iop.org*. **8** 'Wakeham Review', (May 2016), p18. **9** Ibid. p5. **10** Under employment usually refers to employment which the graduate could have done without a degree at all – often a continuation of typical student employment in retail or hospitality. **11** Wakeham Review', (May 2016), p40. **12** Ibid. pp18 & 73. **13** 'Women In Science, Technology and Engineering Campaign', *www.wisecampaign.org.uk*. **14** Equality Challenge Unit, 'Athena SWAN Charter', *http://www.ecu.ac.uk/equality-charters/athena-swan/.* **15** House of Commons Science and Technology Committee, 'Women In Scientific Careers', (December 2014), Houses of Parliament, Westminster.

RESOURCES

The Royal Society for Chemistry – *www.rsc.org/careers*
Institute of Physics – *www.iop.org*
Society of Biology – *www.societyofbiology.org*
Society of Experimental Biology – *www.sebiology.org*
The Sector Skills Council for land-based and environmental industries – *www.lantra.co.uk*
The British Association of Sports and Exercises Sciences – *www.bases.org.uk*
AGCAS Options series – *www.prospects.ac.uk/options_with_your_subject.htm*

PREPARING GRADUATES FOR AN UNCERTAIN FUTURE

1 World Economic Forum, (2016), 'The Future of Jobs: Employment, Skills and Workforce Strategy for the Fourth Industrial Revolution', *www3.weforum.org/docs/WEF_FOJ_Executive_Summary_Jobs.pdf, accessed 29 June 2016* **2** Pathak, P. (October 2015), 'How to future-proof university graduates', *theconversation.com/how-to-future-proof-university-graduates-48639*, accessed 29 June **3** The National Centre for Entrepreneurship in Education (NCEE), *ncee.org.uk/?NCEE*, accessed 5 August 2016. **4** Day, I. and Blakey, J. (2012), 'Challenging Coaching: Going beyond traditional coaching to face the FACTS', Nicholas Brealey Publishing, London. **5** University of Leicester, 'Transferable Skills Framework', *www2.le.ac.uk/offices/careers–new/build–your–skills/skills*, accessed 1 August 2016. **6** WildHearts, *wildheartsgroup.com/micro-tyco*, accessed 1 August 2016. **7** Dweck, C. 'Growth Mindset', *www.ted.com/talks/carol_dweck_the_power_of_believing_that_you_can_improve?language=en*, accessed 8 August 2016

MATHEMATICS, IT AND COMPUTING

1 Department for Business, Innovation & Skills, (May 2016), 'Wakeham Review of STEM degree provision and graduate employability', *www.gov.uk/government/publications/stem-degree-provision-and-graduate-employability-wakeham-review.* **2** Department for Business, Innovation & Skills, (May 2016), 'Shadbolt Review of Computer Sciences Degree Accreditation and Graduate Employability', *www.gov.uk/government/publications/computer-science-degree-accreditation-and-graduate employability-shadbolt-review.* **3** UK Commission for Employment and Skills, (26 October 2015), 'Working Futures 2012-22', *www.gov.uk/government/collections/ukces-sector-insights-reports-2015.* **4** Department for Business, Innovation & Skills,, (October 2013), 'Learning from Futuretrack: The Impact of Work Experiences on Higher Education Student Outcomes', *www.hecsu.ac.uk/assets/assets/documents/Futuretrack_BIS_Learning-_from_futuretrack_work_experience.pdf.* **5** High Fliers Research Limited, (2015), 'The Graduate Market in 2015', *www.highfliers.co.uk/download/2015/graduate_market/GMReport15.pdf.*

RESOURCES

BCS, The Chartered Institute for IT – *www.bcs.org.uk*
Future Careers in Technology – *www.thetechpartnership.com/tech-future-careers*
Institution of Analysts and Programmers (IAP) – *www.iap.org.uk*
Institute of Mathematics and its Applications (IMA) – *www.ima.org.uk*
The Royal Statistical Society (RSS) – *www.rss.org.uk*
The London Mathematical Society (LMS) – *www.lms.ac.uk*

REFERENCES & RESOURCES

ENGINEERING AND BUILDING MANAGEMENT

1 Department for Business, Innovation & Skills, (May 2016), 'Wakeham Review of STEM degree provision and graduate employability', *www.gov.uk/government/publications/stem-degree-provision-and-graduate-employability-wakeham-review*. **2** Report published by the UK Commission for Employment and Skills points out that 43% of vacancies in STEM roles are hard to fill due to a shortage of applicants with the required skills. UK Commission for Employment and Skills, (20th July 2015), 'Reviewing the requirement for High level STEM Skills', *www.gov.uk/government/uploads/system/uploads/attachment_data/file/444048/High_level_STEM_skills_requirements_in_the_UK_labour_market_FINAL.pdf*. **3** 'Wakeham Review', Executive Summary & p72. **4** Royal Institute of British Architects, *www.architecture.com*. **5** Morby, A. (March 2016), 'Budget Analysis: Infrastructure Promises', Construction Enquirer, *www.constructionenquirer.com/ 2016/03/16/budget-detail-infrastructure-promises/*, accessed on 23rd August 2016. **6** 'Construction Industry Trends for Emerging Markets', Accenture, *www.accenture.com/gb-en/insight-achieving-high-performance-construction-industry*, accessed on the 23rd August 2016. **7** Engineering UK, 'Engineering UK 2015: The State of Engineering', *www.engineeringuk.com/EngineeringUK2015/ EngUK_Report_2015_Interactive.pdf*. **8** 'Wakeham Review'. **9** 'Women In Science, Technology and Engineering Campaign', *www.wisecampaign.org.uk*. **10** UK Commission for Employment and Skills, (26 October 2015), 'Working Futures 2012-22', *www.gov.uk/government/collections/ukces-sector-insights-reports-2015*, accessed on 23rd August 2016. **11** 'Engineering UK 2015: The State of Engineering', p48.

RESOURCES

Chartered Institute of Building – *www.ciob.org.uk*
Institution of Engineering and Technology – *www.theiet.org*
Institution of Civil Engineers – *www.ice.org.uk*
Institute of Electrical and Electronics Engineers – *www.ieee.org*
AGCAS Options series – *www.prospects.ac.uk/options_with_your_subject.htm*
Women in Engineering – *www.womeninengineering.org.uk*
Women in science, technology and engineering campaign – *www.wisecampaign.org.uk*

SOCIAL SCIENCE

1 Economic and Social Research Council, 'How social science shapes lives', *www.esrc.ac.uk/about-us/what-is-social-science/how-social-science-shapes-lives/*. **2** Campaign for Social Science, 'What is social science?', *campaignforsocialscience.org.uk/about-us/social-sciences/*. **3** Michael Page, 'Public Sector Market Update Q3 2015', *www.michaelpage.co.uk/our-expertise/finance-recruitment/public-sector-market-update-q3-2015*. **4** Association of Graduate Recruiters , (July 2016), 'AGR survey: Women more likely to get top graduate jobs than men...if they apply ', *www.agr.org.uk/News/agr-survey-women-more-likely-to-get-top-graduate-jobs-than-menif-they-apply#.V6szelsrKUk*. **5** Teach First, 'About us', *www.teachfirst.org.uk/about*. **6** Deloitte, 'The Deloitte Millennial Survey 2016: Millennials' values do not change as they progress professionally', *www2.deloitte.com/global/en/pages/about-deloitte/articles/gx-millennials-values-do-not-change-progress-professionally.html#report*. **7** The Law Society, (April 2016), 'Annual Statistics Report 2015', *www.lawsociety.org.uk/support-services/research-trends/annual-statistics-report-2015/*, accessed August 2016. **8** High Fliers Research Limited, (2016), 'The Graduate Market in 2016', *www.highfliers.co.uk/download/2016/graduate_market/GMReport16.pdf*. **9** Campaign for Social Science, (2015), 'The business of people: the significance of social science over the next decade?', *campaignforsocialscience.org.uk/wp-content/uploads/2015/02/ Business-of-People-Full-Report.pdf*.

RESOURCES

Royal Geographical Society – *www.rgs.org*
Royal Economic Society – *www.res.org.uk*
Law Society – *www.lawsociety.org.uk*
British Sociological Association – *www.britsoc.co.uk*
British Psychological Society – *www.bps.org.uk*

REFERENCES & RESOURCES

ARTS, CREATIVE ARTS AND HUMANITIES

1 Joint Council for Qualifications, (2015), 'Entry Trends, Gender and Regional Charts GCE 2015', *www.jcq.org.uk/examination-results/a-levels/2015/entry-trends-gender-and-regional-charts-gce-2015*, accessed 22 August 2016. **2** Ofsted, (2011), 'Girls' career aspirations', *www.gov.uk/government/publications/girls-career-aspirations*, accessed 22 August 2016. **3** Department for Culture Media & Sport, (2016), Creative Industries Economic Estimates, (January 2016), *www.gov.uk/government/uploads/system/uploads/attachment_data/file/523024/Creative_Industries_Economic_Estimates_January_2016_Updated_201605.pdf*, accessed 22 August 2016. **4** Creative & Cultural Skills, (2015), 'Building a Creative Nation: The Next Decade', *ccskills.org.uk/downloads/CCS_BUILDINGACREATIVENATION_WEB_SINGLES.pdf*, accessed 22 August 2016. **5** Paul Hamlyn Foundation, (2014), 'ArtWorks Evaluation survey of artists', *www.phf.org.uk/wp-content/uploads/2015/06/ArtWorks-Survey-of-Artists.pdf*, accessed 22 August 2016. **6** National Careers Service, 'Job Profiles: Actor', *nationalcareersservice.direct.gov.uk/advice/planning/jobprofiles/Pages/actor.aspx*, accessed 22 August 2016. **7** The Higher Education Academy English Subject Centre, (2011), 'Top ten qualities employers value in English graduates', humbox.ac.uk/2998/7/top_ten_qualities.pdf, accessed 23 August 2016. **8** National Audit Office, (2016), 'Training new teachers', *www.nao.org.uk/wp-content/uploads/2016/02/Training-new-teachers.pdf*, accessed 23 August 2016. **9** Ibid. **10** Office for National Statistics, (2013), 'Graduate in the UK Labour Market: 2013', *www.ons.gov.uk/employmentand labourmarket/peopleinwork/employmentandemployeetypes/articles/graduatesintheuklabourmarket/2013-11-19*, accessed 23 August 2016. **11** European Commission, (2010), 'Employers' perception of graduate employability' *ec.europa.eu/public_opinion/flash/fl_304_en.pdf*, accessed 23 August 2016. **12** Higher Education Statistics Agency, (2015), 'Students in Higher Education 2013/14', *www.hesa.ac.uk/pr211*, accessed 23 August 2016. **13** European Commission, (2012), 'Europeans and Their Languages', *ec.europa.eu/public_opinion/archives/ebs/ebs_386_en.pdf*, accessed 23 August 2016.

BUSINESS AND ADMINISTRATIVE STUDIES

1 AGCAS Editors, (March 2016), 'Accountancy and finance', *www.prospects.ac.uk/careers-advice/what-can-i-do-with-my-degree/accountancy-and-finance*, accessed 25 July 2016. **2** High Fliers Research Limited, (2016), 'The Graduate Market in 2016', *www.highfliers.co.uk/download/2016/graduate_market/GMReport16.pdf*, accessed 25 July 2016 **3** Deloitte LLP, (2015), 'From brawn to brains: The impact of technology on jobs in the UK', *www2.deloitte.com/content/dam/Deloitte/uk/Documents/Growth/deloitte-uk-insights-from-brawns-to-brain.pdf*, accessed 16 June 2016 **4** Association of Chartered Certified Accountants, (2016), 'Professional accountants – the future', *www.accaglobal.com/content/dam/members-beta/images/campaigns/pa-tf/pi-professional-accountants-the-future.pdf*, accessed 2 August 2016. **5** High Fliers, 'The Graduate Market in 2016', accessed 25 July 2016. **6** Ibid. **7** Graduate Recruitment Bureau, 'Industry Profiles: Travel, Leisure and Tourism Industry Profile for Graduates', *www.grb.uk.com/travel-and-tourism-industry-profile#qualifications*, accessed 25 July 2016. **8** AGCAS Editors, (December 2015), 'Marketing', *www.prospects.ac.uk/careers-advice/what-can-i-do-with-my-degree/marketing*, accessed 25 July 2016. **9** Graduate Recruitment Bureau, 'Industry Profiles: Marketing', *www.grb.uk.com/marketing-industry-profile/*, accessed 25 July 2016.

RESOURCES

After English – *www.afterenglish.ac.uk*
Creative Choices – *ccskills.org.uk/careers*
Creative Skillset – *creativeskillset.org*
Dance UK – *www.danceuk.org*
Drama UK – *www.dramauk.co.uk*
The Actors' Guild of Great Britain – *www.actorsguild.co.uk*
The Historical Association – *www.history.org.uk*
Incorporated Society of Musicians – *www.ism.org*